SALVATION
CITY

SALVATION CITY

HALFWAY HOUSE STORIES

JOHN C. KILBURN, JR.
AND S.E. COSTANZA

To all of those fighting the battle of recovery.

TABLE OF CONTENTS

LIST OF FIGURES

List of Tables

ACKNOWLEDGMENTS

The data from this study were collected over many years. We had formal and informal conversations with recovering addicts, people in treatment for mental illness, and former prisoners. We dedicate this book to all of these individuals in hopes that they find happiness. Several drafts of various chapters were presented at numerous departmental colloquia and brown bag lectures, as well as at national and regional conferences. We are grateful for the input from many people who commented on various concepts that we discuss in this book, and we wish to offer special thanks to our colleagues at Texas A&M International University, Eastern Connecticut State University, Central Connecticut State University, Salem State College, Western Washington University, and Louisiana State University. We have benefitted from working with innumerable brilliant colleagues.

Various drafts of chapters received helpful comments, and we would like to single out the significant input from Carl Bankston, Deborah Blackwell, Sandra Garrett, Ronnie Fernandez, Eric Metchik, Frances Rhodes, and Pam Palmer. Additionally, we would like to thank the staff of Teneo Press for their tremendous support throughout the development of this book.

We would also like to acknowledge our wives, Judith Kilburn and Sarah Costanza, and our children, Madeline and Robert Kilburn, as well as Natalie, Wyatt Cashen, and Carter Costanza for their loving support and for enduring the countless hours that we were away from home in completing the research and writing of this book.

PREFACE

By John C. Kilburn, Jr.

The writing of this book was prompted by opportunities that I had to record the experiences of many people who lived, worked, and were rehabilitated throughout the states of Connecticut, Louisiana, and Texas. I heard stories of halfway houses much more complex than the one that is often told in the popular media—that of the simple dichotomy between "bleeding hearts" and "heartless" individuals. The "bleeding hearts" are often portrayed in popular discourse as those who condone spending government funds freely and refuse to make addicts or criminals responsible for their own behavior. The war between these two factions continues in popular culture and dates back to the days of John Howard, the 18th-century Enlightenment philosopher who founded the penal reform movement. Improvement in prisoners' basic rights and their access to proper reformatory care continues to be advocated for today, largely by political progressives. This position involves increased funding of residential facilities for both addicts and people convicted of drug crimes.

The "heartless" individuals are those portrayed as advocating correctional "warehousing," thinking only of their own economic interest and showing little compassion to society's cast-offs. One example of the "heartless" that has been immortalized in literature is the exchange that takes place between Ebenezer Scrooge and two missionaries in Charles Dickens's *A Christmas Carol* (1986 [1843]):

> SCROOGE: And the workhouses? Are they still in operation?
> MISSIONARY: They are.
> SCROOGE: The Treadmill and the Poor Law are in full vigor, then?
> MISSIONARY: Both are very busy, sir.
> SCROOGE: Oh! I was afraid from what you said at first that something had stopped them in their useful course. I am very glad to hear they are still operating.
> MISSIONARY: A few of us are endeavoring to raise a fund to buy the poor some meat and drink, and means of warmth because at this time the want is more keenly felt.
> MISSIONARY: What shall I put you down for?
> SCROOGE: Nothing.
> MISSIONARY: You wish to remain anonymous?
> SCROOGE: I wish to remain alone. I don't make merry myself at Christmas and I can't afford to make idle people merry. My taxes help support the establishments I have mentioned and those who are badly off must go there.
> MISSIONARY: Many would rather die.
> Scrooge: If they would rather die, they had better do it and decrease the surplus population.

For many advocates of community corrections, those that seek to cut funding for progressive correctional programs are modern iterations of Ebeneezer Scrooge. However, it is important to remember that the concerns of homeowners in neighborhoods that are targeted for halfway house siting are based upon a solid foundation. Among residents' primary concerns are personal security (Rabkin, Muhlin, and Cohen 1984), declining property values (Dear 1977; Farber 1986; Myers and Bridges, 1995) and a general negative impact on neighborhood amenities and quality of life in the community (Baron and Piasecki 1981; Eynon 1989).

Also, many such homeowners are rightly concerned with the well-being of neighborhood children. That said, children in neighborhoods that are targeted for halfway house siting also face potential stressors from growing up with a halfway house in close proximity. For example, a newspaper article in the *Los Angeles Times* reported that residents in a Long Beach community objected to the placement of a halfway house in their neighborhood. A six-year-old child stated that "Because of the crazy man house, my daddy won't let me play outside anymore. I don't want to play outside because of those crazy men" (Bailey, 1985).

During my interviews, I heard diverse stories of hope and despair that convinced me that this was more than a battle that could be explained in black and white. I heard stories of recovery and community that were inspiring and needed to be retold in a larger framework. Turning this into a simple battle of right and wrong creates an eternal impasse that does not result in progress in addressing a significant social problem in communities.

My coauthor had the unique experience of moving to an affluent community in central Connecticut around the time of the highly publicized "Petit Home Invasion" (Gandossy, 2010). This home invasion occurred within a affluent suburban community very similar to his own. The link shared by the two suspects in the home invasion was having met in a halfway house in Hartford, Connecticut close to my coauthor's new residence. The home invasion caused a great deal of concern in my coauthor's neighborhood. Among his neighbors, many people spoke of getting new alarm systems, dogs, security lights, and legal permits to conceal firearms. Even in neighborhoods far away, the resonance of the Petit Home Invasion could be felt due to the national publicity.

The experiences shared by my coauthor and myself regarding halfway houses were so divergent as to create tension between us when we discussed the rehabilitative capabilities of halfway houses. We, two researchers, who had worked together on many previous publications, found ourselves disagreeing for the first time on the potential of rehabilitation. After a few conversations, it became apparent that researching policies regarding halfway houses—not just in Connecticut, but in every state—was in order. We agreed that the issue of the halfway house must be revisited. This is an essential step forward in both community sociology and criminology.

In this book we look at some of the benefits that halfway houses provide, as well as some of the turbulence, threats, and perceived threats that they create for communities. On this issue, we agreed that there is no right or wrong, but only the idea that halfway houses are a matter of two facets: social policy and moral good.

Because facilitated reentry treatment for both criminals and addicts into the community is most often devised to result in greater moral good, my coauthor and I agreed that halfway houses are a noble idea in theory. They are, ideally, a righteous concept at both a practical level and a moral level. At a practical level, they strive to facilitate smooth operation of social control agencies such as penal facilities, free up prison space while allowing intensive supervision of parolees, and halt addiction problems before they become legal matters. At a moral level, they represent a noble attempt to facilitate the reentry of ex-convicts, addicts, and the mentally ill into the community as "new" and reformed individuals.

We acknowledge that there are many positive attributes to well-run halfway houses. These are places where convicts or addicts who have been institutionalized and are unprepared to reenter the community can regroup themselves and marshal the resources and state of mind to return to the community. Well-run houses are usually safe residences that social-service-minded providers are assigned to watch on a 24-hour schedule. They act as treatment centers for those with drug addictions as well as those with mental illnesses.

For most people in halfway houses, we express a great deal of sympathy. It is important to remember that those placed by social control agencies in halfway houses must, in most states, meet the criteria of being a nonviolent offender. Those who place *themselves* into halfway houses, such as addicts or mentally ill people, are not at fault for their own condition.

   However, our sympathies go out to communities as well, especially to those without the affluence to fight the placement of halfway houses in their neighborhoods. Communities, in turn, are the topic of this book. In a functional society, any public health service or part of the criminal justice system seeks to protect the community from the criminal or addict that it fears. Halfway houses act, in a sense, as a failsafe device to prevent social outcasts, like those discussed earlier, from reentering the community before they are rehabilitated. These houses offer the hope that the residents of the houses will avoid drifting into the same unhealthy lifestyles that had initially placed them in the institution. Both the halfway house participant and people linked to that person in the surrounding community are affected by the halfway house. For example, when thinking of the halfway house participant, it is important to also think of the business owner who runs a store located across the street from the home. It is also important to realize that it is not only the individual offender or addict suffering. Both the problems and the rehabilitation process of the resident or client affect children, mothers, fathers, siblings, spouses, and extended family. Therefore, the rehabilitation process can do a great deal of good to the extended community network when a client participates in a program that has integrity.

   However, at the same time and for good reason, halfway houses have drawn a great deal of fire from community members who do not want to see them placed near their homes. People who have enough financial resources often fight the placement of transitional residences within their communities. The proximity of perceived societal outcasts harms their property values, heightens their level of fear of crime, and burdens local social service agencies. At this time, we are hard-pressed to see the direct benefit to any residential community of having halfway houses in their area. Although residents of halfway houses may benefit from living in a stable neighborhood, their presence leads to legitimate concerns raised by the neighborhood residents. We hope to present a clear understanding of this problem from various points of view and move towards a solution that leads to the greatest good for the greatest number of people. Although it may be easy to view this social problem as a

simple zero-sum game, where one population gains only when another
group of individuals lose something, we believe there are solutions that
may benefit both residents of halfway houses and the greater communities that host these residents.

SALVATION CITY

INTRODUCTION

One of the most difficult issues related to the study of halfway houses is defining them. Webster's Third New International Dictionary (2002) defined a halfway house as "A residence for individuals after release from institutionalization (as for mental disorder, drug addiction, or criminal activity) that is designed to facilitate their readjustment to private life," but there are so many different variants of halfway houses that one definition may not suffice. For example, in this definition, the dictionary specifies that halfway houses are specific to individuals who have been released from prior institutionalization. This is not always the case, as we found many people that were voluntarily admitted to halfway houses for personal recovery reasons. Others were motivated to admit themselves into halfway houses because they were facing specific legal and/or family issues. Regardless, most halfway houses we visited during our research were used as places to facilitate "getting sober" in order to reenter society.

HALFWAY HOUSES: A TYPOLOGY

In order to clarify the definition of "halfway house" as used throughout this book, we have attempted to create a typology of the halfway house. Throughout the course of this book, we interview people who were released from two types of halfway houses (substance abuse and criminal activity/work-release). We noticed different patterns of admission or commission which can be used as the basis of a classification scheme, including:

1.   Self/Voluntary admission
2.   Commission by a relative or other concerned party
3.   Commission by the state after institutionalization
4.   Commission by the state in lieu of institutionalization

In addition, during the course of our interviews we learned that there were three basic "types" of halfway houses that vary according to type of admission/commission. In the following table, a classification scheme was developed for halfway houses visited during the course of this research. Although we realize there may be other types of halfway houses, such as those that specialize in mental health needs, they were not on the list of those we visited and they fall outside the scope of our current research.

VOLUNTARY-ADMISSION HALFWAY HOUSES

Upon reviewing the history of the halfway house, we find that voluntary-admission halfway houses have been in operation since the 16th century. Voluntary-admission halfway houses are not usually run by the state or facilitated by some kind of government stipend, but rather by charitable individuals or agencies. These are halfway houses that operate under altruistic principles and act as "shelters" for those who wish to check themselves in. A stay there is usually not free of charge, as homeowners usually require some money from clients for the direct maintenance of the home. All of the houses that fall under the category of "voluntary

Halfway House Placement Factors.

Characteristics	Voluntary admission halfway houses	State-subsidized substance-abuse halfway houses	State-subsidized work-release halfway houses
Principal concerns	Principal concern is with sobriety.	Principal concern is with sobriety after prison, or as a diversion of a prison stay.	Principal concern is preventing violations of intensive supervisional parole or probation, or other new criminal activity.
Management	Run independently by altruistic individuals, agencies, or "private entrepreneurs."	Run with state intervention by altruistic individuals, agencies, or "private entrepreneurs."	Run with state intervention or directly by state.
Penalty for violation	Penalty for rule violation is eviction.	Penalty for rule violation may be a forced return to prison for technical violations or return for criminal violation.	Penalty for rule violation may be a return to prison.
Onus of reform	Onus of reform is on clientele who often regulate one another's behavior.	Onus of reform is on clientele who are routinely checked by employed staff members or probation/parole officers.	Onus is not on reform, but on transition to the workplace.
Client composition	Clientele may include individuals genuinely attempting to	Clientele may include individuals in transition between imprisonment	Clientele may include individuals in transition between imprisonment

(*continued on next page*)

Halfway House Placement Factors (*continued*)

Characteristics	Voluntary admission halfway houses	State-subsidized substance-abuse halfway houses	State-subsidized work-release halfway houses
Client composition	become sober or awaiting trial for drug- or alcohol-related offenses.	and work-release houses or directly sentenced individuals.	and free society or individuals otherwise serving a community-based sentence.
Clientele payment	Clientele usually pay on a sliding scale for the direct maintenance of the home.	Clientele payment is variable depending upon the client's legal situation.	Clientele usually pay for the maintenance of the home on a sliding scale as part of punishment and reform effort.

admission" that we discovered were considered substance-abuse rehabilitation facilities. Most people who admit themselves to these halfway houses are seeking to get themselves sober, or to avoid rough patches in their lives when they need a place to stay or face legal entanglements.

Voluntary-admission halfway houses are principally concerned with sobriety. We discovered that these types of houses are usually operated either independently by altruistic individuals or agencies or by private entrepreneurs. Many of these voluntary admission halfway houses operate "under the radar" so as not to alarm neighborhood residents with their presence. The alternative is to ask for a state stipend, which many halfway houses do, at the risk of upsetting local neighborhood residents. Of course, by taking government funds, there is greater need for direct accountability and a more public image. In some ways, voluntary-admission halfway houses seem like a better alternative for communities because they operate quietly. However, in the worst cases, they are run by "slumlords" who are simply looking to profit from the misfortunes of the homeless or substance-abuse victims. Housing is provided to a person that is seeking a low-cost residence.

The penalty for rule violations in most halfway houses that are "voluntary admittance" is eviction. In most of these settings, we discovered that clients often regulate one another's behavior. In other words, they seek to stay sober, and keep each other clean and sober. During our interviews, we discovered that other clients usually evict people who drink or use on the premises of a voluntary-admittance halfway house because they are seen as problems for the ongoing operation of the house.

Clients at voluntary halfway houses may include people attempting to become sober or awaiting trial for alcohol- or drug-related offenses. In some cases, we discovered that people awaiting trial on substance-abuse charges attempted to demonstrate their good standing to the court by temporarily admitting themselves to a halfway house. Prosecutors, especially when drug offenses are considered minor and seen as a product of addiction, will display leniency to people who attempt to reform before trial while charges are pending (Zimring, 1993). One interesting aspect of substance abuse treatment relates to the idea that although affluent substance abusers have the financial ability to check themselves into upscale clinics such as the Betty Ford Center, those from lower socioeconomic status groups may face halfway houses as their only option. We discuss the social justice implications of this in our conclusions.

STATE-SUBSIDIZED SUBSTANCE ABUSE HALFWAY HOUSES

Government-subsidized halfway houses in America have been in development since the mid-19th century, when a group of New England and New York doctors began to petition local governments to build temporary "inebriate asylums for habitual drunkards." The principal concerns for state-subsidized houses are essentially the same as those of voluntary-admission halfway houses with regard to sobriety. However, some states' departments of correction specifically commission subsidized substance-abuse halfway houses to deal with issues of sobriety and community corrections. Therefore, clients of state-subsidized half-way houses may be either admitted or committed. Although it is rare to have both populations mix, it does occasionally occur. For example, the state correctional department may purchase a few beds in a particular halfway house.

State-subsidized substance abuse halfway houses are the most common type of substance abuse halfway houses. They include those more notable and respected houses such as Oxford Houses and their many affiliates, who receive tax subsidies to run their facilities. On the other hand, occasional violations of social justice occur in cases where landowners seek tax breaks for themselves by running state-subsidized halfway houses.

In most of the cases we encountered, there were specific differences between state-subsidized halfway houses that specialized in former convict populations and state-subsidized halfway houses that specialized in voluntary populations. In some ways, many of the state-subsidized substance abuse houses run by correctional departments have a great deal of integrity because they are monitored closely by the state and open to scrutiny from the public. Often parole officers will be assigned to monitor these houses on a twenty-four-hour basis. There are two primary concerns regarding halfway houses. The first is public safety. One of the paramount tasks of state-subsidized housing for former convict populations with substance abuse problems is ensuring that these ex-convicts do not reoffend or become threats to the community around them. The second is sobriety maintenance after prison, which may present a challenge to offenders who are encountering decompression effects after release.

Client demographics for state-subsidized halfway houses may vary from individuals who are relatively affluent to those who have been raised in the worst conditions of poverty. Some clients are in transition between prison and another type of halfway house that specialized in work-release. Other clients are placed in a halfway house as an alternative to formal incarceration in a prison facility.

As is the case with voluntary substance abuse halfway houses, in most state-subsidized substance abuse halfway houses the penalty for rule violation is expulsion, which in the case of a criminal offender or former convict may result in a forced return to prison or to new imprisonment. The onus of reform in most state-subsidized substance abuse halfway houses is on the client themselves; however, unlike those who we interviewed in voluntary substance abuse halfway houses, clientele in state-subsidized substance abuse halfway houses are routinely checked by house staff members or probation/parole officers.

At some levels, the responsibility of the state to financially maintain and subsidize substance abuse halfway houses becomes a social justice issue. Throughout this book we make mention of this several times, pointing out that by taking on the responsibility of subsidizing halfway houses, the state has placed itself in a position where it must at least monitor supervisors, clientele, and operation of the program. We ask, in our conclusions: is it fair to the taxpayer to have to pay for these subsidies?

Clientele in state-subsidized halfway houses may include individuals in transition between imprisonment and work-release houses or directly sentenced individuals. Frequently, parolees and probationers are expected to pay rent on a sliding scale. This may be both to facilitate an ongoing sentence in terms of reparations and to acclimate the ex-convict client to the work environment that he or she must rejoin. Of course, the nature of government subsidies to all types of operations vary depending on the client's legal situation, the type of halfway house operation, and the availability of governmental funds targeted to address the specific social problem that halfway house focuses on.

STATE-SUBSIDIZED WORK-RELEASE HALFWAY HOUSES

Shortly after the Civil War, humanitarian groups developed "Homes for Discharged Prisoners," also called "Houses of Industry." This marked the advent of work-release/criminal halfway houses in America (Wieder, 1988). The original purpose of the work-release halfway house, to aid an individual's rehabilitation as they transition to everyday life in the general population, remains the same today. Such places are often the bane of local communities' residents, many of whom are concerned with how criminal halfway houses in the vicinity will affect their own property values. Often, the placement of criminal halfway houses, like the placement of prisons, jails, liquor stores, or sex offenders, generates a response among community members known as "NIMBY" ("not in my back yard"). The NIMBY response is discussed in later chapters.

The principal concern of work-release/criminal activity halfway houses is preventing violations of intensive supervisional parole (ISP) that criminologist James Byrne (1990) once called a failed "panacea." Violations of probation or other new criminal activity are closely monitored in criminal activity halfway houses, and there is often a set of rules or regulations pertaining to halfway house clientele. Listing each state's provisions would take far too long and exceed the scope of this book; however, each state has their own set of regulations for halfway house residents who are leaving correctional institutions. For example, in Connecticut, clients at work-release halfway houses must fall into a "low risk" category in terms of violent crime and the ability propensity to recidivate.

State-subsidized halfway houses and work-release/criminal-activity halfway houses must be run either with state intervention or directly by the state Department of Corrections. In theory, the purpose of the criminal halfway houses is not specifically reform but rather transition to the "real world." In addition, as with state-subsidized substance abuse halfway houses, the halfway house setting allows parole and probation officers to keep a close watch on clients.

Clients of a work-release/criminal activity halfway house are, of course, never self-admitted. These may include individuals in transition between imprisonment and free society or individuals otherwise serving a community-based sentence. Clients usually pay for the maintenance of the home on a sliding scale as part of the punishment and reform effort.

HALFWAY HOUSES: JUSTICE ISSUES AND DAILY OPERATIONS

The primary goal of any halfway house has always been to ensure the provision of recovery services while regulating the behavior and lifestyle of the resident. Since this crosses the spectrum of serving the mentally ill and those addicted to alcohol and other drugs as well as those facing sanctions from the correctional system, it is challenging to summarize in one document the daily operations of each and every halfway house. There are significant justice issues related to the daily operation of halfway houses.

Because halfway houses may be seen as a public good that benefits society in general by assisting in the rehabilitation of those that are leaving institutionalized settings, it may benefit the general public to provide funds for their operation. Of course, whenever any program is subject to public funding there must be accountability regarding the stewardship of those funds.

Although most of these operations are not directly operated by a governmental agency, government funds pay for their operation. Some are run by nonprofit organizations while others are run for profit. Regardless, there are incentives for providing low-cost service delivery. Many governmental agencies call for the programs they fund to demonstrate accountability. Therefore, the question of whether or not these programs work comes to the forefront.

Nonprofit social service providers usually run halfway houses directly. It is the goal of the halfway house to provide social services for populations that are not able to fully take care of themselves during the period of transition between confinement or addiction and reentry into the community. Although most people would agree that it is necessary for the halfway house to deliver outstanding service, there is the reality of budgetary constraints. These constraints sometimes interfere with appropriate staffing, safety conditions, sanitary conditions, and the integrity of certain behavioral therapy programs. In terms of having a well-qualified and sufficient staff to resident ratio, we must acknowledge that adequate funding is necessary. With regards to safety and sanitary issues in the halfway house, the building must be up to code and the staff must monitor day-to-day operations very carefully. Additionally, the programs aimed at behavior modification, such as substance abuse or anger management programs, must be steeped in principles of integrity (Gendreau, Little, & Goggin, 1996).

Some halfway house programs focus more on safe custody of the clients and therefore offer more structured operations, whereas others are more treatment-oriented and allow residents a significant amount of freedom. One of the difficult issues related to understanding the nature of halfway houses is that each individual residence deals with unique problems and the type of treatment that is most effective will differ. For example, with former prisoners reentering the community through the halfway house, vocational training may be in order. For other residents of halfway houses, addiction and control therapy may be more appropriate. Therefore, we cannot describe the halfway house as using a single approach to addressing the various problems that each individual faces.

This book contains many stories of people who have been residents of halfway house programs in anonymous towns in three different areas of the United States. We have used information from these stories to create "Salvation City" in order to illustrate the very real life problems that exist while maintaining the confidentiality of the interviewees and general anonymity of specific regions and programs. We interviewed residents and former residents of halfway houses. We also interviewed professionals in fields such as substance abuse counseling and parole administration who have experience working with halfway house clientele. Although many of these interviews were recorded as far back as the early 1990s, we assert that public concerns regarding funding, operations, and even justification for the existence of halfway houses has not changed significantly over time.

The research method in this book has been somewhat inspired by authors such as Barbara Ehrenreich (2008) and Elijah Anderson (1999) who have gone out among community members seeking to explore social phenomena. We use narratives of experiences from residents, the general public, and correctional professionals, among others, to explore the cumulative effect that halfway houses have on social actors. In terms of working in the academic community, our professions also allowed us a unique perspective on, as well as access to, these interviews. However, our style and approach attempts to closely follow the work of

Elijah Anderson (1999) because it observes a set of consequences to communities with moral implications.

SALVATION CITY

For illustrative purposes, we have created a single city based on the characteristics of several cities sharing similar characteristics. Although the rich detail is largely drawn from our experience and interviews with residents of three U.S. cities, many of the characteristics of these cities are the stories of many American cities. If one was looking for an ideal community in which to set up a halfway house, one would want to find a community that has housing stock widely available and also an abundance of low cost housing. Since the availability of low cost housing for residents is of paramount concern, areas with multiple residential housing would be preferable. The anonymity of the residents is also essential, so driving by these houses one must see no significant markers that these dwellings are anything other than simple residences.

Based on the ideal specification of characteristics required to make a halfway house successful, we have created a composite of the ideal community for a halfway house that is located in the center of a larger area that we call Salvation City. Each of the towns that make up the composite of Salvation City was once an industrial town that contributed greatly to the US economic boom from the Industrial Revolution through the 1950s. The halfway house district within Salvation City is our model, but it is also quite parallel to one of the communities that we collected interviews from. Only certain neighborhoods within Salvation City contain halfway houses, and as with every American city, a halfway house is a rare phenomenon.

Although most of the excerpts used in this book are based on interviews from three specific cities, it is important to remember that halfway house districts in the rest of the United States are probably *not* as well suited to rehabilitation as the halfway house district in Salvation City. Because of Salvation City's unique history (described in Chapter 3), nonprofit halfway houses probably had an easier time setting up shop in that area than they would have had in most cities. In this book, it is important to remember that we focus on the halfway house in general, its meaning to community (both symbolically and economically), and how it is becoming a matter of sustainability.

CHAPTERS

Chapter One is about sociology, which involves the scientific study of human interaction. In Chapter One, we discuss how the halfway house fits in with philosophical and sociological concepts, focusing on the ideal greater good. We attempt to develop a community sociology perspective using staples from the three major perspectives in sociology: functionalism, conflict, and symbolic interactionism. We frame the issue in this chapter of why understanding halfway houses is important.

Chapter Two describes the history and practical functioning of halfway houses. Although the focus of our interviews remains the ideal community for rehabilitation via the halfway house, we felt it necessary to give a thorough description of the halfway house and its historical development. A discussion of the historical development of halfway houses leads to a discussion of their current purposes. We also discuss different types of halfway houses in the ideal operational mode.

Chapter Three describes the history of Salvation City, our ideal typical town for the rehabilitation of halfway house clientele. But the "tale of Salvation City" is actually a "tale of two cities" because of the dichotomy between neighboring affluent communities and struggling communities. This situation is not uncommon in the United States. Such a city is perhaps best typified in the city of Flint, Michigan, whose struggles with a bifurcated economy were well documented by the director Michael Moore in the documentary *Roger and Me*. Many residents claim that Salvation City may be described as a community that has the potential to remain prosperous after the decline of local industry. They may think of Salvation City as "The Land of Opportunity." However, others describe Salvation City as a place that began to see its economic fortunes dwindle after the decline of the city's industrial base, subsequently becoming known as a dumping ground for the region. The lower class district of Salvation City is understood by residents as a place where "welfare mothers," people with mental illnesses, and the general underclass go to struggle with survival issues.

As with Flint, Michigan, there is some validity to both versions of the city history. The town boomed with the development of industry that came into existence during World War II, bringing many outside migrants into the area to meet labor needs. After the closing of many businesses during the 1960s and 1970s, there arose several issues with substance abuse in the area. "Boom and bust" cycles going back to the Industrial Revolution and continuing through World War II have plagued Salvation City, just like many other American cities. The city centers were once known as entertainment and shopping districts. The areas where the houses are located were the residences of once-proud families expecting upward socioeconomic mobility. The majority of individuals with the economic means to relocate have moved to the suburbs or neighboring towns.

Chapter Three also discusses the problem of community decay that came along with the decline of jobs in the inner city, as it became a chronic social malaise in communities throughout Salvation City. Scholars such as Douglas Massey and Nancy Denton (1993) as well as William Julius Wilson (1987) highlighted the idea that the decline of the industrial base of several cities has led to a restructuring of community to the point that many former industrial cities have become defined by patterns of community decay. The book *Disorder and Decline* by Wesley Skogan (1990) also provided an in-depth analysis of why such decay occurs based on an analysis of economic cycles. Substance use and abuse has always been a part of the culture of Salvation City. There are numerous legends and histories that describe Salvation City as a regional hub for the distribution of drugs even before the decline of area industry. This problem has led to a troubled existence for many communities in the area. Although local efforts to fight addiction in the area have been pursued for many years, the problem of high addiction rates persists.

Chapter Four describes the need for, and benefit of, halfway houses. More specifically, it describes why the halfway house district of Salvation

City is an attractive location for a significant cluster of these programs. In the chapter, the nature of program integrity is discussed along with a discussion of what halfway house residents go through in their daily life. In this chapter we also define the ideal halfway house resident. Salvation City offers many advantages to the ideal resident due to the location of cost-effective and quality social services. Because of this, there is a tendency for halfway house clientele who rehabilitate in Salvation City to not recidivate upon reentry. In this chapter, we discuss the many success stories of halfway houses in Salvation City with an emphasis on the idea that if program integrity is maintained and location is ideal, halfway house rehabilitation is a boon to both the community and the resident.

Chapter Five describes the shortcomings of halfway houses in a community sociology context. The chapter begins with a discussion of the Cheshire home invasion, which made national news in the summer of 2007. Although it is important to point out the positives of halfway house programs for both offenders and communities, it is also important to point out the negatives of the halfway house as a strategy for reentry or addiction cessation. In the case of the Cheshire home invasion, we find that the halfway house is an ideal meeting place for criminal minds and observe the argument that the failed outcome of many halfway house programs may result in extremely dangerous situations for communities

Chapter five also observes the "NIMBY" phenomenon. NIMBY is an acronym for "Not In My Back Yard," which has come to be a common theme in more affluent areas that can afford to resist the placement of halfway houses. In Salvation City, we discovered that community resistance to halfway house siting is a much more complex issue than shortsighted heartlessness or prejudice. Many people love the traditions of Salvation City. Several individuals discussed pleasant memories of a time in the recent past where people shopped and the focal point of family entertainment was Main Street. The Downtown Theatre, the fountain exhibit, the Mayfair Parade, and other events prompted the gathering of citizens from all communities in Salvation City to an area near the halfway house district. It is here that the effects of the halfway houses are most likely to be felt by residents of Salvation City. The downtown area was once a community that was perceived as safe and a place where every modern amenity was offered. It was "high living" at its finest. These halfway houses are blamed for much of the decline of downtown life.

Chapter Five also addresses the idea that public concern about dangers of halfway houses may be more perceived than actual. The chapter asks whether or not these social misconceptions are indeed social problems: "Do real community problems accompany the existence of these houses?" According to many of our interviews, they do cause some problems. However, we find that many of the people interviewed have solutions to these community problems.

Chapter Six, which contains our conclusions, discusses how halfway houses may be reconciled with local communities. Some of the potential solutions to the problem of siting recovery houses may be solved through more intensive supervision, programs with more integrity, appropriately staffed programs, and well-maintained halfway houses. We also address problems with fiscal austerity and sustainability with regard to continued government support for halfway houses. One common debate that we observe is currently taking place across the United States and involves cost-benefit analyses of deconcentrating social services and recovery homes. We revisit the effectiveness of programs, such as the Connecticut Payment in Lieu of Taxes (PILOT) program and Fair Share agenda on the reconciliation of community with halfway houses. The possibility of rewarding communities that deal with a disproportionate number of social problems is also explored in our conclusions. Communities that carry a significant fiscal burden are not yet fairly compensated.

In our conclusions, we also explore the nature of social organization in communities. Our discussions with various halfway house residents, social workers, and people that reside in neighborhoods near halfway houses allowed us to examine issues of collective consumption, culture, and politics as they affect communities. As a warning, we point out that continuing the simple debate of the "bleeding hearts" versus the "heartless" will likely yield no progress in the future. It is necessary to explore their arguments in depth in order to understand the nature of this problem.

CHAPTER 1

A STORY OF INCOMPATIBLE GOODS

DEVELOPING A COMMUNITY SOCIOLOGY PERSPECTIVE OF THE HALFWAY HOUSE

Any time you go and apply for a job and you check that application, you see that little box that says "have you ever been convicted of a felony?" and sometimes that's hard for people, really hard for people, man.

—Luis Fernandez

In part, this book is the story of two unique types of communities and their specifically convergent issues. Because the issues regarding ex-convicts reentering the community are pandemic, it is also the story of many other places. It is a story of drug use and blighted neighborhoods; a story of gated communities and green suburban utopias; however, at a more abstract and general level, it is a story of what happens when criminal offenders, psychiatric patients, and drug addicts attempt to reenter the communities that once rebuffed them.

The issues regarding halfway houses illustrate a much larger, yet all too commonly overlooked, dilemma in human societies. That dilemma is the existence of incompatible moral rights. The search for the ideal and the "greatest good" are frequently invoked as justifications for policies and actions. Policies geared to facilitate the greater good, therefore, are often misguided. Furthermore, when it is commonly accepted that they are not facilitating the greater good, such policies are too often thrown away quickly and without regard for the consequences. Public policies regarding halfway houses, institutions that are maintained in every state to facilitate the needs of offenders returning to the community, are the framework for the issues discussed in this book.

The intellectual historian and political philosopher Isaiah Berlin suggested that pluralism is a fundamental fact of our social condition. By pluralism, he did not mean that there is no objective truth or that people simply differ in their preferences and in their interpretations of events. Berlin meant that there are often multiple and competing moral goods (Berlin, 1953). This can be an argument for an ethic of liberal tolerance, and Berlin meant it to be so (Berlin, 2002). The philosopher Alfred North Whitehead, who argued that all things are morally relativistic, also shared this opinion. We feel that such a discussion applies to the halfway house and its implications for communities because such a discussion involves both the potential for rehabilitation, which positively affects society as a whole, and the placement of halfway houses, which affects communities in a negative way.

Philosophers such as Berlin also noticed that competing moral goods are frequently mutually incompatible. Achieving one desirable end, such as the rehabilitation of the offender, requires sacrificing another equally desirable end, such as the perceived need of community residents for safety. The pursuit of the ideal is one in which the "greater good" leads to sacrificing another great good. Through an in-depth examination of the matter of reconciliation between halfway houses and communities, we offer a concrete example of how Berlin's idea of incompatible moral goods is very relevant to today's society.

Moral goods, such as community-based rehabilitation of social outcasts and perceived well-being of communities, may be incompatible on logical grounds. Berlin noted that liberty and equality, for example, are inconsistent to the extent that equality hinders liberty, or that liberty hinders equality. Incompatibility between moral goods is also often rooted in conflicts of significance between interacting interest groups. The interests of one group of people, such as halfway house residents, may be fundamentally at variance with the interests of another, such as residents of any given community. Similarly, the interests of one course of action meant to facilitate the needs of a certain segment of the population (for example, criminal rehabilitation) may require sacrificing the interests of another equally valuable course of action.

There are many issues brought about by debating moral goods that are relevant to community sociology. In this book, we ask the question of whether society in general must move toward well-organized communities at the expense of human rights. At one level, we observe that the intention of any community-based residential correctional facility is to create a buffer between the public and the criminal it fears. At another level, we observe that in the process of reconciling the social outcast with the community, there are many dangers that present themselves. Similarly, we observe that the intentions of drug treatment program residences and mental health residences perform a valuable function in sequestering unhealthy people from the rest of society. However, we also observe how the placement of such residences may interfere with the perceived well-being of the collective community.

Functional government must observe communities' rights to be protected, because a functional community must feel (although not necessarily achieve) a sense of security and well-being. It is unquestionable that every resident has that right. At another level, many human rights advocates argue that a completely functional community is an ideal that cannot be achieved and must be left in check to serve the greater good, which represents rehabilitation of all offenders at the national level. Justification of the search for the ideal has resulted in both many atrocities and many tremendous leaps of mankind throughout human history. Public goods regarding who pays for something, who benefits, and who bears the burden of programs meant to serve the greater good will always be a foundation of political debate. There are many social problems or situations in which competing actors can claim to have "justice," "reason," or "right" on their side.

In discussing the greater good of global rehabilitation, it is necessary to discuss the individual communities and people who, some would argue, represent a "lesser good." State-sponsored facilities ostensibly serve the noble ethos (good) of rehabilitation (Wexler, Falkin, & Lipton, 1990), often helping substance abusers overcome addiction and/or transitional criminals on community release find a viable occupation (Martin et al., 1999). However, while the general public shows support for the tax incentives that accompany deinstitutionalization (Gray, Conover, & Hennessey, 1978), negative community reaction to transitional housing is almost a given (Piat 2000a). Communities support deinstitutionalization economically and philosophically, but take exception to both real and perceived negative community impacts such as diminished housing values and heightened crime rates (Kim, 2000). While such transitional facilities simultaneously represent state-sponsored efforts toward easing taxpayer burdens and rehabilitation, communities often understand halfway houses as an affront to common good (Orndoff, 1978; Piat 2000b).

Two mutual goods that are of paramount concern—community security and reform efforts—are thrust into the limelight in this book. Our criminal justice system, along with our healthcare system, has made mission statements visible to the communities that they promise to serve. However, a mission to reform addicts, offenders, and mentally ill people is often at cross purposes with the perceived well-being of community members.

The criminal justice system seeks to reform the offender so that he or she may reenter the community with little or no damaging consequences. Likewise, many agencies affiliated with healthcare have made a commitment to return people who are either mentally ill or are addicted to substances to the community with little or no damaging consequences. However, when such people, who are designated as social outcasts, do return to communities, there is often a sense of fear that accompanies disagreement about how they should return and where they should return to. There is also the ever-present debate on whether actual rehabilitation takes place in community-based treatment or correctional programs.

There are few places in American society where conflicting moral goods are easier to see than in the situation of the halfway house. Most

Americans would probably agree that the idea of community-based transitional housing for society's outcasts is a noble idea, in theory. However, in practice, most Americans would probably agree that the idea of placing a community-based correctional or treatment facility in their own neighborhood is not desirable. So, with that in mind, there remains the lingering question of "where should these people be placed?"

In the chapters that follow, we examine the compatibility of the moral goods of both community-based rehabilitation and communities that are focusing on the halfway house as a paramount concern. Discussion of this issue is important in terms of economic discourse because the issue of halfway houses becomes a sustainability issue in the sense that halfway houses present a suitable avenue to reducing the costs of rehabilitation. Because federal, state, and local governmental agencies demand accountability for every dollar that is spent in correctional and rehabilitation programs, the development of an efficient reentry program is necessary.

Such a discussion involves the consideration of the halfway house as a potential method of alleviating the fiscal responsibility of the overburdened American correctional system for incarceration, which now oversees the management of nearly 7,000,000 individuals (including those incarcerated, on probation, on parole, or otherwise serving alternative sanctions). Droves of ex-convicts may return to society because there is simply no funding available to build prisons and employ new prison staff. Similarly, the option of expensive health care treatment for the mentally ill or drug-addicted is becoming less and less of a reality. This makes halfway houses, which are run as a public service either by government agencies or individual interest groups, a key issue for future sociological research.

SOCIOLOGICAL PERSPECTIVES ON THE HALFWAY HOUSE

Struggling to be value neutral, the sociological study of community problems rarely takes these kinds of fundamental conflicts between moral goods and interests seriously. This is understandable because concepts such as "the greater good" are not empirically observable, nor are they amenable to quantitative testing. The question of halfway houses is an ideal battleground with which to frame such an issue. Generally, those who write about social problems tend to present them as if every difficulty could be solved with the right laws, right social movement, or the right economic system. It behooves us at this point to observe how competing traditional perspectives on sociology, which is the scientific study of social interaction, might view the halfway house as a social phenomenon. In his discussion of the dilemma of social services' impact on society as a whole, Peter Rossi (1978) described the problem of the "social minima" and the "societal minimum." The term social minima refers to the idea that everyone should have reasonable life chances with regard to employment opportunities and health. The societal minimum acknowledges that the unemployed, the unrehabilitated, and those who are debilitated by substance abuse are not contributing to the welfare of others in the larger society. Many individuals believe that members of society should care for each other and offer services to those in need of assistance, but the question of where to locate those services is constantly under discussion. The term NIMBY is frequently used to describe a situation where many support the services but do not want the services located in their neighborhood. "Not In My Back Yard" has a rich and growing literature (Bohon & Humphrey, 2000; Cowan, 2003; Matejczyk, 2001; Wilton, 2002). Another term for this phenomenon is the "LULU problem" ("Locally Unwanted Land Uses"). There is general consensus regarding the need for factories, chicken farms, power plants, and halfway houses. Some acknowledge that each of these must exist in order to gain their benefits (jobs, business taxes, electricity, or a better-functioning public).

However, there are concerns that some towns bear more than their fair share of these LULUs. Although some communities in close proximity to transitional residences may have correctional institutions and psychiatric hospitals, clients under their supervision rarely go out in the general public. In addition, few people have ever stated that they enjoyed a psychiatric hospital or prison so much that they decided to stay around the area after they were released. Satellite aftercare and post-release community supervision is provided throughout the state. However, there is a widely held sentiment that halfway houses are importing people with many social problems who are harming the community.

Rossi (1978, p.577) claimed that "the establishment of a human services delivery system rests upon a number of critical assumptions, as follows:

1. There are deficient individuals, households, or institutional arrangements. These deficiencies prevent optimal functioning of some individuals and households. Furthermore, the presence of these individual and/or institutional deficiencies in the society presents problems to the society.
2. If the deficiencies can be corrected or compensated for, functioning can be changed so that individuals and households can function "normally" through the use of some sort of human service "treatment."
3. The human services "treatment" can be delivered uniformly and widely through the training of delivery personnel and through the placement of them in the organization.
4. There are no serious conflicts of interests between the social control goals of human services and the goals of clients.

Rossi claimed that "the evaluation of human services delivery systems ordinarily takes place around points two and three." Therefore, evaluating halfway houses in terms of how to fund them, what to expect in terms of treatment methodology, and where funding may exist will continue to be addressed in this book.

FUNCTIONALIST PERSPECTIVES ON HALFWAY HOUSES

The functionalist perspective of sociology is taken from the early works of Emile Durkheim (1997[1892]), a French sociologist, who believed that all institutions (such as the halfway house) naturally evolve to meet the inherent need that society has for order. From the functionalist perspective, halfway houses are naturally evolved products of the social order and exist because they promote social order. In this sense, any social malady brought about by the existence of the halfway house, such

as rising neighborhood crime rates, can be attributed to poorly functioning halfway houses and/or extraneous macrosocial influences that lead
to such poor functioning.

Historically, the necessity for halfway houses has been well documented.
As American prisons began to meet their nominal operating capacity during the 19th century, there arose a need for intermediate correctional facilities. Because, in American correctional policy, the onus has historically
been placed on rehabilitation, it was logical that such places also provide
a rational plan for "farming" the offender back into the community. In
addition, because one of the paramount functions of the criminal justice
system is also to provide a buffer between the public and the criminal that
it fears, it was a rational step to develop such places in such a way that the
transitioning offender would be sequestered from the community.

Therapeutic halfway houses (for those who are not directly adjudi-
cated by the courts), which developed in America during the temperance
movement of the mid-19th century, also served the function of maintaining order. Although they developed free of the constraints of the criminal
justice system, such halfway houses serve a similar function in terms of
sequestering the addict or alcoholic from the larger community. A functional program is one that provides adequate supervised custody, treatment, and successfully manages the reentry of its clientele. It can be
argued that one of the latent dysfunctions of such arrangements is that
they create a great deal of community unrest and disruption to the collective conscience of neighborhoods in which they are placed. This book
shares the archived experiences of many individuals whose lives have
been changed, for better or for worse, because they used specialized
programs to learn how to live in society. We will also share the experiences of many community members who experienced the halfway
house as a disruption and a threat.

We chose to begin our presentation with the story of a former pre-
scription-drug addict who benefited from a successful program, Jane.
Jane, by all accounts, is the ideal halfway house success story. In her
case, neither community nor addict suffered any ill effects from the
results of halfway house activity.

JANE'S STORY

One successful case in which both halfway house client and community reaped the benefits of the halfway house was that of a former prescription drug addict, Jane. She was originally placed in a psychiatric hospital after overdosing on prescription medication. Her present-day appearance is one of maximum functionality. The case also provides evidence that a detoxification in the hospital followed by simple outpatient treatment without the structure and support offered by a halfway house would be ineffective.

At the time of her archived interviews, Jane was about nineteen years old and living with her boyfriend. She had participated in outpatient treatment designed specifically for drug addicts. By all accounts, Jane is petite and has an angelic face. Based on appearance alone, she would not be the type one would suspect of having addiction problems. She is now very active in political affairs and community service as well as in caring for her young child, Carlton.

Her recovery home treatment plan offered her a structured environment that was safe, a strict set of rules guiding her behavior, and access to intensive counseling. Jane's story illustrates a key facet of any functional program, which is integrity. When discussing questions regarding her overdose and institutionalization, Jane was very open and spoke highly of her experience with halfway houses. Of the terror of being hospitalized for an overdose, she said the following:

> There are certain points when you are pushed too far and anybody would react. But that doesn't mean you are psychotic. And the worst thing I remember about [the hospital] was that you overdose then they bring you to the hospital then they pump your stomach.
> (Personal interview: Jane)

Jane went on to say that at the hospital, she had to sleep on the floor because they did not have a bed. She was bombarded with numerous questions from staff during her detoxification process:

> It wasn't bad but the next day they bombard you. I mean I just tried to wreck my body and it's like ninety-nine people come up

to you and they give you this insane several hundred question bubble thing and it's like do you like sports? How often did you try to commit suicide? Are you blonde?

Jane discussed the stigma attached to recovery. She claimed her turning point toward recovery treatment was finding the right counselor, who placed her in the right halfway house program:

> I think he just taught me that he was there and that was weird because there were so many people who said if you need help, come to me. And when you'd come to them, they'd just throw it back in your face. They would either punish you for coming for help or they'd hold it over your head or turn you into a charity case.

While the safe environment and readily available treatment assisted in her recovery, Jane stated that transitional living was essential after treatment. She stated that:

> It's weird to be taken away from your normal environment to learn how to function in it while you're not there. I mean, one finger if you want to answer and two fingers if you have a question. Keep things in a locked cabinet and everything comes in a container like you're having meals on a flight.

From a functionalist perspective, there is an obvious question that develops from stories like Jane's: If halfway houses are so good at facilitating recovery, then why has there not been an overwhelming body of supportive evidence obtained through sociological research? The answer to this question is possibly that some halfway house operations are more effective than others and thus display a greater degree of functionality.

Dysfunctional halfway houses may operate in such a manner that a substantial proportion of their residents recidivate, either through committing technical violations (violations of contractual terms with either the residence or state) or new violations. This may be due to a failure in halfway house preparation and management of offenders or to a larger dysfunction of the social order, wherein halfway house staff may be operating under a restricted budget.

Dysfunctions in halfway house preparation and management of offenders are frequently mentioned in the general media. One example that we highlight in Chapter Four is the case of a Cheshire, Connecticut home invasion in which two former halfway house residents committed murders. This case became a center of attention in national and local media.

There are many other cases in which halfway houses have inappropriate bedding, heating, inadequate transportation to and from work, unusual odors, and plumbing problems. Inadequate funding or maintenance by the state or other agency that runs the halfway house is usually the cause of such halfway house problems. The ideal goal of penal and therapeutic halfway houses is an issue that we seek to address fully in this book.

From a functionalist perspective, halfway houses and failures related to them might also represent a schism in the social order that is not easy to detect. Failures in today's halfway house system might be due to the simple economic fact that residents of halfway houses cannot make enough money to survive upon reentry to society. We recognize the importance of the economy in this matter. Unemployment and other issues, such as the rising price of commodities, prompt us to believe halfway houses are a sustainability issue for modern America.

CONFLICT PERSPECTIVES ON THE HALFWAY HOUSE

Conflict theorists, borrowing from the works of Karl Marx (1997 [1848]), recognize that conflicts of interest exist between all subgroups in society. Conflict theory claims that in any given society, one group's set of interests always conflicts with "social justice" and therefore true "social justice" cannot easily be achieved. In this sense, halfway houses, like correctional institutions, are another means of orchestrated sequestration.

Conflict theorists have long observed potential relationships between socioeconomic inequality and interaction with the criminal justice system. The deinstitutionalization of many psychiatric patients led to specific regions being called "dumping grounds." The concept of the "dumping ground" provides a means to separate haves from have-nots. Such segregation may be apparent in the abundance of formerly institutional-ized people being released to the general community. These people need a place to live and seem to concentrate in certain regions. For example, the Bowery section of New York was called a "dumping ground" when many people were released from the New York State Hospital (Reich & Siegel, 1978). The fact that halfway houses are often relegated to inner-city neighborhoods is a sign of disparity in power. Communities that do not have the socioeconomic power to decline or resist the placement of the halfway house in their area are often victimized.

If the criminal justice system exists as a buffer between mainstream society and the criminal that it fears, then it becomes more apparent why lower-class inner-city neighborhoods are most often "stuck with" the placement of halfway houses. Although generally the outcomes of halfway house treatment are globally felt, it is highly unlikely to find a halfway house in a neighborhood with the aggregate financial means to politically resist.

The conflict perspective brings up further debate when one considers the issue of rehabilitation and proximity to lower-class inner-city areas. Segal, Baumohl, and Moyles (1980) report that only certain communi-ties have the means and political voice to unite in opposition against half-way house placement. Kraft and Clary (1991) and Hunter and Leyden (1995) suggested that responses to transitional housing may represent and small, but vocal minority. Such a perspective suggests that wealth or income could play a role in the prevention of transitional housing place-ment within communities. Literature on social justice confirms that lower class neighborhoods often become dumping grounds for undesirable populations, but such communities are often unsupportive in addressing the needs of recently released offenders (Grygier, Nease, & Staples Ander-son 1970; Hardwood, 2003; Listwan, Colvin, Hanley, & Flannery, 2010).

There is further concern, from the conflict perspective, that the placement of halfway houses is a constructed product of an upper-class-controlled zoning system. As a result of these financial issues, there are many people who complain of addiction and recovery houses harming the natural charm of neighborhoods and communities, but only a small number of communities have the fiscal austerity to resist the placement of such homes.

A former staff member of a treatment program, David, was asked if concerns about community politics were legitimate. David, an anger management counselor, defended the integrity of well-managed programs against local public sentiments:

> Absolutely! I can't beat around the bush—I mean they need to practice common sense. There's a lot of drug addicts in this town, and active drug addicts do bad things. Recovering addicts that are doing the right things, you have nothing to worry about and they're probably better people than the people writing letters [complaining to their congressman].

Furthermore, halfway houses, when presented with challenges by their community, must defend the issue of their own integrity. David, in an archived interview, stated:

> Many people in treatment are very serious about their recovery and wish to live a peaceful life. We have people with problems, I mean a lot, a lot of problems [...] maybe not paying their child support [...] Things that need to be reconciled [...] A lot of legal issues come in there, a lot a lot of legal issues. Maybe they are not paying child support. We get some dual-diagnosed people that we are really not qualified to handle. One time we had a gentleman that was overweight. And we said just substance abuse: we don't want to hear about overeating or gambling. If it's not substance abuse, it doesn't go in our treatment plans and it doesn't fit in our scope of treatment.

Due to the nature of opposition from fiscally affluent neighborhoods, conflict theory also leads us to take note of the issue that halfway houses are often under-funded and synonymously placed in lower class urban areas. This leads to several problems with program integrity that cannot be ignored.

Jimmy, a client of an inner-city halfway house, became the victim of a brutal assault in his own treatment facility. Jimmy, a 45-year-old who was five foot seven inches tall and nearly 200 pounds, was furtive and found it hard to share his story. Records indicated that because of funding problems with the halfway house that Jimmy was residing in, there was a problem with understaffing. Jimmy recounted one story in which he was assaulted and a staff member could not be found for almost an hour:

> I was on the back porch talking on my cell-phone. It was the other guys that called 911. They [the paramedics] asked the guy [the assailant] and he denied it. Some of the guys said "we're from prison, we don't rat on anybody." But there were some other people that hadn't been in prison so they don't know that mentality so they reported that it was an unprovoked assault. I was unconscious. I didn't even know it was coming. It came from my back. He hit me with a chair and I hit the radiator at the wall with my head.

From a conflict perspective, the residents of halfway houses are society's underclass that experience disproportionate placement in correctional facilities. Most likely, halfway houses are filled with residents who are from low socioeconomic status areas and, when facing prison release or addiction problems, are simply rerouted to other poor areas. Other problems with treating halfway houses as warehouses and the communities that surround them as dumping grounds may include exposure to open-air drug markets, street corner gambling, and prostitution. In addition, such disempowerment may include a willful negligence by police officials and patrolmen to provide security to halfway house areas.

Because of such conditions, many residents fail to reform, and it becomes an awkward legal concern when an individual violates the rules set by a halfway house. One social service provider, Peter, discussed his frustrations with attempting to provide services to a group of individuals that sometimes "get it" and sometimes "don't." He stated:

> People need to get serious, because so far, my experience is that some people are not serious about getting the job done. Because

I have been involved with calling people about some of these illegal activities, even inviting myself to see the detectives and [Salvation City] police because I see what is happening under my own nose. I mean, I see those residents dealing, and I'm calling the place to talk to a detective and they never see me.

Peter understood what was going on in disenfranchised neighborhoods. When asked about why he was not more vocal about his concerns, he stated that politics play a significant role in his job and he does not want to "rock the boat." He also mentioned that the safety of his family, as well as his own personal safety, was a significant issue related to speaking out too much against drugs. Violence is often part of the drug trade and people that cause problems for the business can get hurt.

LOCATION, LOCATION, LOCATION

The success of those who enter halfway houses in disenfranchised areas is also limited by their potential exposure to the same kinds of conditions that got them involved in crime in the first place. Transitional housing is needed for society. However, at the same time it is obvious that in neighborhoods where it is placed, residents become anxious over real or perceived security issues. Similarly, although transitional housing is often placed in communities that already have stagnant economies, it is arguable that the presence of the halfway house further reduces fiscal austerity within communities. Helping addicts or ex-convicts reintegrate into society, therefore, may lower the crime rate, but it still can ruin the businesses of shopkeepers. On this issue, equally desirable goals are utterly at odds. To examine such issues, it is perhaps best that we turn to conflict theory.

People residing in higher-value communities argue against halfway houses' placement there based on two arguments: first, that it is more costly to operate these houses in more affluent communities; second, that more affluent people pay a disproportionate share of taxes and their property values may suffer by having offenders residing in their part of town. It is difficult to ignore the merits of the conflict perspective on social policy when it comes to the placement of the halfway house. Furthermore, affluent communities have often organized themselves to petition town councils not to allow zoning of halfway houses in their neighborhoods. Such a phenomenon is recognized in popular and academic discourse as NIMBY (Not In My Back Yard). Conflict theory draws attention, and rightfully so, to the fact that halfway houses tend to be placed in communities that are already rife with crime and deep into disorder. Specifically, it is of interest that the geographic placement of such houses is normally in neighborhoods with low economic status, low levels of education, high percentages of renters, and a great degree of family disruption (according to census statistics).

SYMBOLIC INTERACTIONISM PERSPECTIVES ON THE HALFWAY HOUSE

Symbolic interactionism is another perspective that can be useful in examining halfway houses. Symbolic interactionism, an idea first put forth by George Herbert Mead (1934), emphasizes phenomena regarding learning and labeling. The first issue involved in a symbolic interactionist approach is learning. Criminal offenders might go to halfway houses and possibly absorb criminal knowledge from other offenders that they meet. Similarly, drug-addicted clients might learn ways to rationalize their addiction through extended contact with other addicts in a poorly staffed situation.

We followed the case of William, an automotive mechanic who was a 42-year-old resident at a drug addiction halfway house:

> "That's all that was there was a bunch of other addicts. Sometime some of the inpatients would even smuggle in some stash. I met at least two connections for pot while I was in there."

Of specific concern here is the "cultural importation hypothesis," which is often applied to prisoners and jails (Clemmer, 1940; Thomas & Foster, 1973). The cultural importation hypothesis suggests that the bringing together of many people from troubled backgrounds may precipitate a subculture prone to criminality.

Within the bounds of a halfway house, individuals sharing the desire to get clean and sober might reside together. One individual's relapse can serve as a negative influence to the others in the home. One individual told a story of a house that fell victim to a "domino effect." This individual, Harry, relayed a story about a resident who brought crack back to the house.

Harry, a 53-year-old male who looked somewhat older than his age, went through the revolving door of recovery many times. Harry got on his feet, only to relapse. He had worked to pay rent to live in a group home, had recently gained transportation by purchasing a bicycle, and was performing successfully on the job at a local supermarket.

The nature of Harry's relapse begins with the story of community within the home. Harry lived with a group of other addicts who were heavily reliant on one another for support within their own milieu. For example, they would cook together, eat together, and do laundry together, among other things. Though residents sometimes had a television of their own, they shared their television with others. In another example, when one individual received an unexpected financial bonus, he purchased steaks to share with the other members of the house.

However, in another instance, according to Harry's interview, one individual relapsed and brought crack back to the house. Unfortunately, this event led to another relapse for Harry as well as for the other five residents, who were removed from the halfway house. Harry had no children, no parents, and only an estranged brother, so the brunt of his relapse affected himself and the community.

Harry's case was no ordinary relapse because he was a success story waiting to happen. His gregarious personality and good nature brought inspiration to all those around him in the community. As Harry was getting out of his addiction problem, he became a local fixture. He was always polite to other residents of the community. After Harry's relapse, however, Harry had difficulty maintaining his social image. He had become estranged from his brother, from whom he often attempted to borrow money. The issue of his brother was a sore spot for Harry, because his brother led somewhat of a charmed life, being a successful businessman and having a family of his own.

I thought I was fooling people. I went from someone who would buy people breakfast to borrowing twenty bucks to score crack. After people realized I was addicted again, I was very embarrassed. I was really embarrassed to show my face around the people I owed money to, so I would often avoid them.

It is clearly in the best interest of any facility to keep this type of story from the public. But, it would be foolish to think that all individuals remain clean and sober throughout their stay. In addition, it is not in the best interest of other residents to allow one individual that is actively drinking and using drugs to remain in the home.

Symbolic interactionist approaches are also concerned with the phenomenon of labeling. From a symbolic interactionist perspective, those who reenter society are doing so with a stigma. Goffman defined a stigma as a socially constructed definition of an individual based on their physical, behavioral, or social traits (Goffman, 1963). In this case, offenders are seen as undesirable neighbors and employees and are viewed as less likely to contribute. To reenter society with the label creates a pigeonhole that the rehabilitated person clearly fits into.

In Harry's case, he discovered it hard to eat at local restaurants even before his relapse, feeling as though people were laughing at him or otherwise slighting him. People often showed Harry disrespect, or so he perceived. This is not hard to understand. Even when Harry was in recovery, he dealt with some stigma. Occasional teasing about his bicycle, working at a supermarket at his age, working as a stock boy, and having a supervisor that was younger than him and critical of his work were part of what was experienced by Harry:

> I couldn't stand the guy [my supervisor]. He was young enough to be my son. I used to tell him that I try to do everything to his specifications. But he used to get on me for not being fast enough.

All three of the major perspectives in sociology provide an impetus for a unified theory of the halfway house and how it fits in with community. The concepts can be unified in to form an integrative perspective. From a functionalist perspective, it can be seen that halfway houses are indeed a logical step in the evolution of traditional correctional institutions and other forms of confinement. From the conflict perspective, knowledge is gleaned that confirms that halfway houses will most often be placed in troubled socioeconomic areas and underfunded due to political circumstances. From the symbolic interactionist perspective, one can see that learning and labeling are two problems that transcend aggregate conditions such as economy or polity. A unification of these theories under the umbrella of community sociology provides a unique jumping-off point from which to research the halfway house.

DEVELOPING A COMMUNITY SOCIOLOGY PERSPECTIVE: WHY UNDERSTANDING HALFWAY HOUSES IS IMPORTANT

The most obvious answer to why understanding halfway houses is important is that understanding halfway houses allows us to explore the connections between rehabilitation and community in detail. Community sociology, due to its emphasis on general interaction outside of a grand theoretical proposition, provides a jumping-off point that allows us to draw from the three major sociological theories.

From a functionalist perspective, halfway houses are simply understood as an evolved form of intensive supervisional parole that takes a heavy-handed approach to reintegrating offenders during the reentry process. It is clear that the American public supports being tough on crime, and there is substantial support for well-monitored rehabilitation programs (Applegate, Cullen, & Fisher, 1997). From a conflict perspective, one can look at the selective placement of halfway houses into communities that might indeed serve some people more than others. Finally, from a symbolic interactionist perspective, one can seek to further understand the concepts of learning and labeling as they apply to (or interfere with) rehabilitation and reentry.

From a community sociological perspective, the understanding of the halfway house is extremely important for numerous reasons, including the rehabilitation effort that goes along with the attempt to reenter the community. First, because halfway houses often have impacts on the

neighborhoods where they are placed, community sociology is concerned
with the effect of the halfway house on the neighborhood. It is important
to observe the interaction effects between residents of the halfway house
and the local community. Second, it is important to focus on the interaction between community residents themselves because the placement of
the halfway houses often affect local morale. The possibility that halfway
houses may be a negative catalyst of community change in terms of crime
rate, property value, and general quality of life must be considered.

Accordingly, community sociologists and criminologists are interested in the idea that halfway houses may potentially affect both real
and perceived community safety. There is much in the literature that
indicates that perceived safety among neighborhood residents is more
important than real safety. Community sociology takes into account that
such perceived security issues should be taken as a priority of the rehabilitation effort.

While a well-run halfway house program may be very effective in the
rehabilitation of offenders, thus making society safer, it may do immediate damage to communities in terms of lowering perceptions of quality
of life. Social decay theorists such as John Stark have pointed out in the
literature that moral cynicism plays a great role in cycles of urban blight.
Such perceptions may work to lower property values and contribute to
rising crime rates caused by residents' unwillingness to get involved in
community affairs.

Of course, from a conflict perspective, an integrated community
sociological theory can borrow the idea that affluent communities are
the least likely places for halfway houses. We acknowledge that inner-
city communities or areas otherwise disenfranchised become the target
of placement practices. Neighborhoods with the financial and political
strength to fight the placement of the halfway house are often free from
government influence in siting issues.

Along with such abstractions such as the perceived quality of life
issues, community sociology takes into account the more concrete issues
of property values and costs of rehabilitation. When visiting the issue
of where these halfway houses are located, the cost of rehabilitation

becomes a substantial concern. In order to offer services in a cost-effective manner, these halfway houses are often relegated to low-rent locations. However, by concentrating these operations in a low-rent region of a state, residents of those regions can complain that the "dumping" of social services in their community may lead to an overwhelming concentration of offenders residing in their town.

Finally, community sociology is interested in both rehabilitation and in the fact that halfway houses may provide it, eventually leading to safer communities. Treatment that addresses antisocial behavior and family relationships seems to show significant success (Andrews & Bonta, 1994; Dowden & Andrews, 1999; Sherman et al., 1998; Simourd & Andrews, 1994). What works in terms of rehabilitation is well-known. Numerous studies led to the detailed development of the Correctional Program Assessment Inventory (CPAI) developed by Paul Gendreau and Don Andrews (1996).

However, there are two issues that develop from this research on rehabilitation. Investment in a well-run program is costly because there is significant need for a well-trained and stable team of treatment specialists operating these treatment programs (Martin et al., 1999). A well-run program that operates on a large scale must hire accountants and compliance personnel to ensure that tax dollars are used effectively. A bureaucracy delivering treatment to offenders who are at-risk develops into a complex operation.

A UNIFIED THEORY OF HALFWAY HOUSES

This book is not so much about criminal justice or corrections, but relies heavily on a community sociology approach. There are some basic principles that provide the foundation for this book. One is that rehabilitation of criminal offenders is a public good. The philosophy of community corrections has shown that work-release programs and halfway houses can benefit offenders and lead to lower rates of recidivism

We concede that poorly run programs offer little benefit to society and, as the case may be, do considerable damage to neighborhoods where halfway houses are placed. This book seeks to not only examine the effect of the halfway house on the community but also the effect of the halfway house on the offender, who returns to the community during the reentry process.

From a community sociology perspective, we address the multiple services needed to examine offender rehabilitation. Such intensive reentry interventions must deal with a great deal of adversity. This adversity varies according to various types of offender populations and community placement.

In developing an ideal examination for effective halfway houses, four primary factors (see Table 1) should be taken into account: risk (the potential risk that halfway house residents present to the community around them); needs (the level of services needed by each halfway house resident in order to succeed in reentry); treatment (the idea that each individual has their personal set of strengths and weaknesses, so treatment must be responsive) and community resources (which often vary).

All of these factors must be taken into account when offering effective treatment to offenders residing in halfway houses. Our approach

TABLE 1. Table of factors to be taken into consideration when considering appropriate halfway house placement and clientele.

Risk	Needs	Treatment	Community resources
If someone is a serious risk to the community, then prison may be the best place for them. We do not believe that community release is the best method for all offenders.	Each individual has their own set of strengths and weaknesses. Some of these issues might have to be addressed to reduce the likelihood of recidivism.	Types of treatment vary in effectiveness. All three of these factors (mental illness, substance abuse, and criminality) must be taken into account when offering effective treatment to offenders residing in halfway houses.	Each individual community has strengths and weaknesses. Some communities have better access to jobs, health care, and a large population of skilled treatment specialists.

offers critical insight into what the halfway house is and into what must be done in order for it to work as a viable social policy. We feel that this is incredibly important. It is important because the halfway houses, at some level, involve sustainability issues.

As more and more offenders reenter the community, it is necessary to negotiate positions on the halfway house that are both viable and actually facilitate such reentry. We agree with the functionalist perspective that halfway houses are naturally evolved products of the social order, but we also feel that there may be many dysfunctions. Although some of these dysfunctions may be explained away as simple failings of the halfway house themselves or even failings of the economy, we adhere to the conflict perspective that proposes that halfway houses are a matter of failed social justice.

Underlying this concrete study of an urban problem is an anti-utopian perspective on human society. The suggestions at the end of the book are not solutions, but compromises that seek to minimize damage and to reach an imperfect but livable state. In describing the difficulties of this community, we hope to provide some insight into just how intractable these troubles are and to offer some thoughts on better approaches to them than are available at present. But, we also want to give an example of a true conflict of interest in American society and to ask readers to think about how many similar situations abound in our nation and in our world.

CHAPTER 2

THE DEVELOPMENT OF THE HALFWAY HOUSE

HISTORY AND PHILOSOPHY

In the introduction to this book, we use Merriam-Webster's definition of a halfway house in order to establish common ground for the reader. However, through extended analysis, it becomes apparent that the dictionary definition of the term "halfway house" may present problems for historical research. In England, for example, this term is often used to refer to psychiatric institutions. In America, it is probably most often associated with places where ex-convicts are allowed to dwell. Because the term halfway house has been applied arbitrarily throughout the years to many different types of residencies, there is a gap in the historical research.

Although we acknowledge this unfortunate gap, we feel that it is most important for the reader to recognize the philosophy of the halfway house. Ideally, it is a place that attempts to aid people who are generally thought of by the community as "desperate." As is the case with most modern halfway houses, the philosophical emphasis of the halfway house has always been on transition. During the Elizabethan era, poorhouses were understood as places of transition because they were only temporary residences for people in poverty looking for work. Today, drug addicts, ex-convicts, and those that were previously treated for psychiatric disorders all reside in halfway houses with the hope that after a temporary period of residence in a halfway house they can return successfully to the community.

In America, the origins of the first Temperance Movement (early 19th century) and the end of the Civil War (1860-1865) are associated with the emergence of halfway houses. Globally, however, there is no commonly understood starting point for the halfway house on any continent. Because halfway houses have operated under various names throughout the years ("recovery houses," "poor houses," and "sober houses"), it is hard to find a consummate history of the halfway house that shows one singular, finite place at which the halfway house began. In addition, because many halfway houses throughout history have been run by charities that have sought no endorsement of their actions, their origins also remain unclear. Historically, it is possible that places such as monasteries, nunneries, and convents served functions like providing temporary housing for the disabled during the Middle Ages.

It is somewhat easier and more practical, for the purposes of this book, to attempt to track down the origins of halfway houses in America. The most likely starting point for the halfway house in the United States is in about 1812. At this time, Dr. Benjamin Rush, an American temperance pioneer, proposed that alcohol-addicted persons should be guided by courts for commitment to "sober house hospitals" for periods of inpatient residential treatment (Hall & Appelbaum, 2002). However, it was not until 1830, when the Connecticut Medical Society, presided over by Samuel Woodward, called for the establishment of medical asylums to treat "inebriates." There remains a further 15-year gap between Woodward's call for temporary residences and the establishment of such facilities. It is most likely that the first predecessor to the modern halfway house in the United States was either Washingtonian Hall, founded in Boston in 1845, or Hopper Home, founded in New York in 1845.

It is likely that the emergence of pure correctional residential facilities (or those focusing explicitly on criminally involved residents) in the United States began after either the first wave of Irish immigration (1840 to 1850) or after the end of the Civil War (Barnes & Teeters, 1959). During the mid-to-late 19th century, criminal halfway houses, also known as Houses of Industry or Homes for Discharged Prisoners, were developed by prisoners' aid societies with the principal intention of keeping ex-prisoners out of poverty and therefore out of situations in which they could become involved in crime.

The basic philosophy of the halfway house has not changed much to this very day. A consummate history of the halfway house is presented below. It illustrates that even the legalities surrounding the provisions of social welfare have not changed very much in the last few hundred years (although the delivery has changed). Historically, laws regarding social welfare have been the subject of moral debate. We began our analysis in Elizabethan England. Laws preceding the development of transitional housing were largely a governmental effort to control the disenfranchised and keep order within communities.

HALFWAY HOUSES: HISTORY AND INNOVATIONS

Philosophically, the halfway house is a place that symbolizes an intermediate step between institutionalization and freedom, with rehabilitation and reintegration as its goal. A cursory knowledge of historical events is perhaps necessary if the reader is to understand the origins and development of halfway houses. From these early residences came the philosophy of today's criminal halfway houses, substance-abuse halfway houses, and mental treatment halfway houses recognized today as a staple of community corrections.

POORHOUSES, WORKHOUSES, AND SOBER HOUSES

Perhaps the appropriate place to look for the philosophical origins of the halfway house is in Elizabethan England (1558–1603), where the concept of the "workhouse" was established (Longmate, 2003; Higginbotham, 2006). The workhouse, as it was first established, can be viewed as a precursor to the modern halfway house. Prior to the Age of Enlightenment (circa 1637–1800), in 1572, the Elizabethan Poor Laws were enacted in England to provide relief for the socially marginalized and needy. However, the law suggested that changes be made at the parish level, and parishes of the Church of England took the lead in active funding of contractors to develop and operate workhouses. However, the major effect of the act was not to construct places of relief, but simply to remove traveling beggars from parishes they were not native to.

The 1601 Act for the Relief of the Poor provided the first mention of residential relief for the poor in the form of poorhouses and workhouses (Charlesworth, 2010). The law mandated that each parish appoint "overseers" to ensure that the sick, poor, and elderly received financial compensation. "Idle Poor," meaning those who were of able body, however, were immediately to be sent to a House of Corrections. At this time, Bridewell Groom and a few other houses of correction existed in the United Kingdom. Distribution of funding for the sick and elderly poor often took place in the local churches, where records were maintained. Still, there was no mention in the act of residential relief for those who were both able bodied and homeless.

Some scholars argue that the first workhouse partially focused on offering residential relief for out-of-work persons was founded in Abingdon, England, in 1631 (Higginbotham, 2006). However, it was another fifty-five years before the first British workhouse of note, the Bristol Workhouse (1697), was commissioned by Parliament. In 1723, Knatchbull's Act allowed parish governments to build workhouses without consultation with Parliament (Higginbotham, 2006).

The Enlightenment, a revolution in social thinking that occurred during the late 18th century, brought about a great deal of concern for the quality of life of societal rejects, including the poor, criminal, and mentally unstable. This era also brought about societal criticism of the way that these people were treated by society and government. It was during this time period that great penal reformers such as Jeremy Bentham (1748–1832) and John Howard (1726–1790) sought to bring a wise sense of social justice to all forms of corrections. Although most of their work did not directly focus on halfway houses, it can be argued that the changes that they made in penological thinking contributed to the development of the modern halfway house. Howard and Bentham advocated proper sanitation in facilities, programs meant to develop the vocational skills of convicts, and a powerful religious or spiritual regimen within correctional institutions (Riechel, 2002). The outcome of John Howard's and Jeremy Bentham's criticisms prompted changes in laws and regulations.

RESIDENTIAL RELIEF FROM THE ENLIGHTENMENT TO THE AMERICAN PENAL REFORMATORY ERA

By 1782, there was tremendous pressure on the British Parliament to pass acts that acknowledged the need for residential relief among marginalized segments of the population. Gilbert's Act of 1782 made it possible for certain parishes to unite to build workhouses with taxpayer funding (Slack, 1990). These workhouses provided residential relief for the mentally ill, children, and the aged. For those of "able body," the managerial staff of the workhouses was instructed to provide work.

The early 19th century saw resident workhouses established in Southwell by Rev. J. T. Becher (Marshall, 1961). The workhouse segregated male and female prisoners and did not allow the use of alcohol or tobacco on the premises. It became the model for workhouses across the country. Conditions in the workhouse were harsh, but residential assistance was provided for those who accepted staying. The Middlesex County Asylum in Hanwell, founded in 1831, also acted as a residential assistance facility for the insane. Unlike conventional asylums, the Middlesex Asylum held true to a "non-restraint" philosophy, which suggested patterns of progressive treatment involving the interaction of magistrates mandating specific treatment. This idea of judicial decision-making interacting with residential confinement and treatment was revolutionary (Suzuki, 1995).

From 1832 until 1834, Prime Minister Earl Grey and the Parliament enacted new revisions to the Poor Laws that formally established that able-bodied people outside of workhouses could no longer receive government relief. Conditions in workhouses, which were meant to function as a general deterrent to poverty, were becoming overcrowded themselves.

As is the case with today's halfway houses, residency in a halfway house was usually accompanied by stigma and a low sense of self-worth. Workhouses became known as "pauper places," where residents would suffer in physical, spiritual, and psychological ways. Residential assistance came with a price, much like today's halfway house system. People living in these halfway houses, or pauper places, were required to pay a percentage of what they made at work. In such a way, the dysfunctional halfway houses that developed in mid-19th century England came very much to resemble a "barter system" of residents in that the residents often found themselves stuck in a situation where their income was insufficient to leave the halfway house.

EARLY AMERICAN HALFWAY HOUSES

For many scholars of penology, the history of American corrections consists of five distinct eras: the penitentiary (1780–1830); the reformatory (1830–1890); the industrial (1890–1930); the medical (1930–1970); and the post-Martinson (1970–present) (Reichel, 2002). During the penitentiary era, America began to build its first penitentiaries. They were largely designed according to prescribed methods from British authorities such as John Howard, who held that prisons should isolate prisoners during confinement to maximize rehabilitative efforts. Prisons were to be sanitary, focused on reform, and centered around the idea of turning social miscreants into respectable, hard-working individuals. Because of its emphasis on maintaining silence among prisoners, this approach to corrections prompted the building of several single-cell establishments. One of the most well-known early penal establishments in the United States was the Virginia State penitentiary, built in 1800 and based on Jeremy Bentham's "Panopticon" design (Reichel, 2002). Bentham's Panopticon provided a specific architectural layout for prisons in which each prisoner was to have a separate cell. Cells were to be laid out in a circular formation with a guard post in the center.

There is some evidence that indicates that the first model of the criminal halfway house was actually built during the penitentiary era (Stevens, 2007). During the early 19th century, Massachusetts prison reformers attempted to establish temporary residential housing for destitute former prisoners. According to Stevens, however, the idea failed because the "…Massachusetts Legislature felt that promoting common living arrangements for offenders would enhance crime" (p. 375). In essence, the Massachusetts Legislature felt that prisoners living together in shared quarters would tend to "contaminate" each other. This reflects one of the philosophical staples of John Howard's and Jeremy Bentham's ideas regarding the maintenance of prisoners in solitary confinement and silence.

In the United States, three historical events made it necessary to further the development of halfway houses during the reformatory era. The first of those events involved Irish, Italian, and eastern European immigration, which brought with it a torrent of illiteracy, homelessness, and minor crime. It was during this period that the United States experienced its first problems with overcrowding in the national court system and penitentiary system. The second event that influenced the development of the modern halfway house was the temperance movement, which brought with it a wave of concern about social problems associated with addiction. The third event involved a general philosophical shift from a punishment model to a rehabilitative model among policy makers. All of these events are discussed below.

THE EFFECTS OF 19TH CENTURY IMMIGRATION ON THE DEVELOPMENT OF HALFWAY HOUSES

Between 1840 and 1860, more than one million Irish immigrants, mostly illiterate and with illiterate children, flocked to the United States (Takaki, 1993). In the inner cities, such as Boston and New York, the modern street gang began to emerge from the unemployed Irish underclass. The Irish (who were forbidden by the 1695 Penal Act to receive an education, inheritance, or hold political office) brought with them to America a sense of independence, but also arrived unpolished and illiterate. There is some evidence that the Irish immigrants were not able to find fair employment in the United States due to the discrimination against Catholics among private employers—"No Irish Need Apply" (Jensen, 2002). Many of them sought a better life, but their history with the British did not encourage many to trust the government. In order to practice the Catholic Mass in Ireland (which was forbidden by the British), many of these Irish immigrants formed "secret societies" that had a built-in disdain for governmental authority. This propensity for secretive alliances would play no small part in the development of early American street gangs.

Perhaps because of often being illiterate, unemployed, and impoverished, many Irish immigrants also tended toward alcoholism. This has not been established for certain, however. Many sociologists and historians have argued that the key social problem of immigrants and alcoholism was formed by nativist sentiments, and therefore that alcoholism among Irish immigrants was more perceived that it was real (Gusfield, 1966). Whatever the case, it is possible that a socially perceived need for temporary residencies became a paramount subject of social discourse because of Irish immigration.

From 1860 to 1910, the wave of Irish immigration was followed by a wave of southern and eastern European immigration which bore similarities to the Irish influx. Among the southern European immigrants were over two million people of Italian heritage, many of whom were from areas of Italy where it was conventional to solve problems without government intervention or help. Among the eastern European immigrants were another two million who were mostly Jewish and Polish. These immigrants were often on the run from political persecution.

With each new wave of immigrants, the nature of crime changed and homelessness increased. Crimes such as hooliganism and street fighting could not be dealt with in traditional penitentiary fashion. There were suddenly more criminals than the small penitentiary system of the growing country was able to handle. Fiscal constraints, such as those brought on by westward expansion and then the Civil War, also made it unfeasible to continue building long-term penitentiaries to house this new breed of criminal. Due to the illiteracy among these immigrants as well as to their socioeconomic status, the arrival of these immigrants also probably prompted public changes in the perception of alcoholism. The immigrant waves affected both the penological and medical communities, prompting thought about new strategies.

THE TEMPERANCE MOVEMENT AND ITS EFFECT ON HALFWAY HOUSES

The American temperance movement, although it dates back further than the mass waves of immigration discussed in the previous section, may not have had the same effect on criminal halfway houses as it did on sober houses and predecessors of today's drug rehabilitation halfway houses. The American temperance movement actually began with Dr. Benjamin Rush, who in 1789 founded a temperance community based in the New England area (Levine, 1978). Rush's beliefs led to the development of the concept of preventative education in the United States, although the American Temperance Society, which eventually consisted of over one million members, was not formed until several years later, in 1826.

According to Gusfield (1967), the definition of the drinker as an "object of social shame" began in the early nineteenth century and reached full development in the late 1820s and early 1830s. Gusfield suggested that temperance organizations during the 19th century did not achieve immediate legitimization but instead had to accrue social legitimacy as more and more people were warned about the dangers of alcohol.

This process took several years, but by 1870 mainstream America had accepted a predominantly "dry" attitude toward alcohol.

By the 1850s, the idea that insobriety was a disease, which could be treated through inpatient or outpatient therapy, was beginning to take hold. According to Baumohl (2006), early halfway houses for drunkards and substance abusers were either privately or publicly run. These residencies were known as either "inebriate asylums," which usually referred to residencies established by governments, or "retreats," which were largely run as private services and descended from a therapeutic tradition of temperance.

A society known as the Washingtonian movement, also referred to as the Washingtonian Temperance Society, was established in 1840 in Baltimore, Maryland. This group was best known for its focus on the individual alcoholic and emphasized the need for treatment over abstinence for the greater good of society. The Washingtonian movement's effects can be seen in the development of some of America's earliest retreats and inebriate asylums. Influenced by the Washingtonian movement, there were at several treatment institutions established by 1857, including Washingtonian homes that opened in both Boston and Chicago. However, due to popular sentiments, mostly regarding the idea of helping the alcoholic (an unpopular theme among many temperance leaders), the Washingtonian movement eventually dissolved. Thus, retreat-style residencies constructed to help the alcoholic were mostly funded by charitable organizations.

Although short-lived, the Washingtonian movement also had an impact on the establishment of state-funded inebriate asylums and retreats. A well-documented early example of a publicly funded inebriate asylum is the New York State Inebriate Asylum, established under a New York State charter by an entrepreneur named J. Edward Turner. Thomsen Hall and Appelbaum (2002) described the New York State Inebriate Asylum, founded in 1864, as an idyllic setting for recovery and, in theory, preparation for a return to the community. The asylum is the first known state-funded residential facility singularly committed to the treatment of substance abusers. According to Thomsen Hall and Appelbaum (2002, p. 39):

The private facility was funded by shareholders, among who numbered ex-presidents, former Supreme Court justices, and other political luminaries. Turner's grand designs refer to a "castellated gothic" structure with a chapel seating 500, a winter garden, bowling rooms, and Russian baths.

Another early incarnation of the "inebriate asylum" was the Inebriate Home of Long Island. Although the public asylums seemed like a noble concept, there were often problems with defining legal obligations and limitations of such places. For example, one of the earliest pitfalls of these temporary residences was the idea of forced participation in rehabilitation and a client's right to reject aid from the state. In addition, another common complication recorded with early inebriate asylums was peoples' families' rights to protest their treatment as sick individuals (Valverde, 1998).

Although coerced care at publicly run institutes historically presented many legal problems, other approaches, developed with less of a custodial vision and more of a voluntary nature, continued to develop. One prime example of a voluntary approach to providing residential treatment was used by the Godwin Association, which acted out of the Franklin Reformatory Home for Inebriates in Philadelphia during the 1870s. The Godwin Association would occasionally patrol the streets of Philadelphia for homeless alcoholics and offer them residential assistance (White, 2001).

Around 1875, the Salvation Army, founded by John Booth in 1867, opened several "homes for drunkards," rekindling the humanitarian spirit of the Washingtonian movement. In the following years, residential treatment or temporary housing facilities for alcoholics or drug abusers began to appear all over the American landscape. It was also during this era that halfway houses became popularly associated with post-release and early release corrections.

THE SHIFT FROM A PUNISHMENT TO A REHABILITATIVE MODEL

A final important event that influenced the modern halfway house was a philosophical transition in correctional thinking that began to affect policymakers and ordinary citizens during the mid- to late 19th century. Prior to the mid-19th century, policymakers had mainly regarded crime as a matter of rational choice. There was a focus on punishing criminals as opposed to rehabilitating them. During the late 19th century, penal reformer Walter Crofton experimented with a new system sometimes referred to as the "Irish system" (Riechel, 2002). The principle of the Irish system was to reward inmates on the basis of good behavior in prison. The system had some success; and, partly due to the social conditions that gave rise to halfway houses, an idea emerged that ex-convicts (especially small-time criminals) could be rehabilitated or reformed.

At this time, a positivistic view of crime emerged and influenced the birth of the modern halfway house. Facilities that were traditionally set up to house the homeless and the poor became a resource for correctional officials seeking to facilitate rehabilitation in the aftercare stage of punishment. One example of such a home was Isaac T. Hopper's halfway house in New York, established in 1845 to assist female former prisoners who were seeking to land back on their feet. Immigration during the late 19th century also drew public attention to the suffering of immigrant women—particularly Irish women, who had come to the United States in greater numbers than Irish men (Takaki, 1993). The situations of these women drew public attention to the plight of impoverished women in need of aftercare. The Shelter in Detroit (a halfway house for women and wayward girls), established in 1868, and Rutland Corner House in Boston, established in 1877, were among the first temporary correctional residential facilities in the United States. These shelters often included laundries and sewing rooms to facilitate vocational training.

During the late 19th century, the view that alcoholism was a treatable disease began to gain popularity among both temperance leaders and American officials. The belief that crime often did not happen of a person's own accord was also emerging. Due to such philosophies, halfway houses became fully integrated into the correctional system during the late 19th century. In 1896, Hope House, one of the most famous of old halfway houses, was established in New York. By 1900 halfway houses existed in almost every major city across the country, including Chicago,

New Orleans, Boston, Philadelphia, and San Francisco (Stevens, 2005). Although many of these early attempts at establishing halfway houses failed because of lack of funding and "contamination" beliefs ("contamination" is a process by which inmates wanting to rehabilitate are corrupted by the values of inmates who are not serious about rehabilitation; it is one of the oldest ideas in penology and the basis for solitary confienement), some halfway houses continued to run under the auspices of private donors or philanthropists. Still, at this time halfway houses lacked a great deal of specification within their mission statements. Many of them intended to serve clients such as ex-convicts, addicts, and mentally ill people without attention to proper staffing.

The idea that halfway houses should become increasingly complex in order to serve diverse populations of ex-offenders began to take hold among penologists around 1900. However, during the Great Depression, the actual physical establishment of halfway houses suffered due to lack of financial support. By the 1950s, America had become a very prosperous country and there was much funding became available. Again, perhaps because of new ethical and moral concerns brought about by scientific advances, philosophy continued to shift towards rehabilitating the substance abuser or reforming the prisoner. There was a great deal of concern with the well-being of juveniles during the 1950s as well, and by 1961 federal funds were provided to advance the building of halfway houses for youth offenders.

From 1950 to 1970 both criminal and substance abuse halfway houses were, like the correctional system, dominated by what is commonly referred to as the "medical model" of corrections. The idea that crime and substance abuse were diseases and might be treated as such was further advanced by the popularity of psychoanalysis and by innovations in medical science, such as lithium (Cade, 1949). Explanations for crime and substance abuse that acknowledged genetic or hereditary factors were becoming quite popular not only in the medical community, but, due to the growing literacy of the American population, in popular perception as well.

The halfway house, whether correctional or rehabilitation, came to thrive on philosophies regarding deviant behavior as a form of illness. During these decades (1945–1970), halfway houses became a prime opportunity for outcasts seeking to become reintegrated into society. At this time, it was not uncommon to see halfway houses, such as Synanon House (Janzen, 2001), emerging as therapeutic communities. Within the walls of Synanon houses, established in 1958, there was strict adherence to rules and a strong emphasis on spiritual principles. Additionally, some halfway houses offered valuable opportunities for vocational and educational training, transportation services, medical aid, and even recreational services.

The prototypical model of the halfway house for ex-convicts was Brooke House, established in 1965 in Boston. Brooke House offered an alternative strategy of community release for convicted offenders. Residents of Brooke House were granted access to the community as they endeavored to improve their vocational or employment opportunities. Brooks House also provided a support staff to former convicts to aid in their rehabilitative efforts. A scientific study conducted in 1976 indicated that the majority of ex-convicts who successfully completed Brooke House did not recidivate (Beha, 1976).

In 1967, the President's Commission on Crime and the Administration of Justice provided massive federal stipends to halfway houses that were aimed at facilitating reintegration. The Oxford House network of recovery homes was adopted by others as the model for well-run halfway houses focused on addiction and alcoholism problems. Oxford House was founded in Washington, DC for alcoholics and drug addicts and has become the prototypical model of the "community treatment center." The house operated using democratic principles and was financially self-supporting. Individuals staying at Oxford House were required to pay a reasonable rent on a sliding scale and expulsion was a remedy for relapsing into alcohol addiction or drug use. Peer pressure among residents was also used as a subtle tool to encourage cooperation in the rehabilitation effort.

HALFWAY HOUSES DURING THE POST-MARTINSON ERA

Despite the documented minor successes experienced by Brooke House and the Synanon models during the restructuring phase of halfway houses, the idea of the halfway house was dealt a death blow in the mid-1970s. The famous criminologist Robert Martinson (1974) published his landmark article "What works? Questions and answers about prison reform," which became largely interpreted as a universal condemnation of correctional experimentation. In 1974, a popular misunderstanding of the research conducted by Martinson added fuel to what has now become known as the "penal harm movement." The penal harm movement emphasizes intentional negligence in the maintenance of correctional facilities in order to maximize the punishment experience. In terms of personal culpability, many people believe that individuals should be responsible for their own circumstances. This philosophy argues that criminals made bad choices and that they should pay, that the drug addict should never have taken drugs, and that the mentally ill person needs to work harder in therapy to fix themselves.

Martinson's research, which was in fact a call for deinstitutionalization, became popularly misinterpreted as a statement condemning rehabilitation and all efforts to facilitate it. Since the 1980s, an emphasis on the punishment function of the criminal justice system has overshadowed the function of rehabilitation. Halfway houses, like prisons, have come to serve a "warehousing" function. The development of halfway houses was also hindered during the 1970s by recession and rising energy prices. Although the recession arguably ended during the 1990s, a pattern of streamlining became popular in American corrections during the 1970s and continues to be influential until the present. For correctional halfway houses, developments during the last four decades have meant the loss of benefits such as adequately trained staff, sanitary conditions, and vocational and educational training programs. In substance abuse treatment housing, Oxford House remains the model for sober living. There are currently more than 1200 Oxford Houses in 39 states across 263 cities (www.oxfordhouse.org). The Oxford House webpage reports that more than 10,000 recovering individuals currently live in Oxford houses.

CONCLUSIONS

It is important to look at the history of halfway houses in order to understand popular sentiment and how that popular sentiment interacts with
attempts to provide residential treatment for societal outcasts. In each
decade, problems of crime, drug and alcohol addiction, and even mental
illness are addressed differently by public concerns. In the beginning,
halfway houses were brought about by social attempts to control segments of the population. As history progressed and as America grew, a
newfound perceived need to protect the unprotected and the ill arose in
society. For brief moments in time, residential treatment centers have
received support. Halfway houses apply to the sociological in that they
affect the community and various quality of life aspects.

This book is primarily concerned with two types of halfway house: the
criminal halfway house and the substance abuse halfway house. Today,
the criminal halfway house lies in a tattered state due to both lack of
public support and governmental inability to finance changes in halfway
houses. Government is a large voice, but does not operate in a vacuum.
Government agencies are motivated to respond to public outcry. During
the 1980s, there was an outcry for tougher corrections. The government
began to redefine the (originally therapeutic) purpose of the halfway
house as a correctional matter. What was first a therapeutic approach to
reform has now been replaced by "warehousing." This is especially evi-
dent in correctional residential facilities that are kept in worse states than
prisons. Many of the convicts that we interviewed saw some halfway
houses as an extension of prison. Some even confessed a refusal to stay
there at first, citing horrible living conditions as their primary reason.

Of course, although usually outside of corrections and within the private sector, there are some high quality halfway houses that continue to
operate for substance abusers or psychiatric patients. However, houses
with integrity in their program structure are usually private and not
forced upon people by the state. Staying in this type of house is usually
a matter of choice for individuals who can afford to live there.

CHAPTER 3

SALVATION CITY

CASE STUDIES

Salvation City has a rich history dating back to the Revolutionary War. Its growth as a powerful industrial city followed several economic cycles of growth and decline. The city, which once was an important northern manufacturing center, experienced the same pattern of decline as the inner-city regions of many Rust Belt and New England cities. Such towns are now significantly less central to the modern United States economy.

Today, cheap laborers across the globe now make the products that were once made in these factories, taking the place of the migrant that once lived in Salvation City. No longer is Salvation City the "promised land" for prosperity. Like so many other American cities, Salvation City's communities have suffered because of industrial restructuring, with factory employment moving first to cheap labor sources in the South and, now, overseas to Asia. The economic base for the town's communities has affected the tax base for the city in general. With a depleted tax base came the decline of community resources such as local schools, parks, and other culturally rich aspects of community life.

Of course, this decline did not hit Salvation City uniformly. Like most US cities, certain communities are still intact. These are the communities that are well maintained and are located in an area called the "Garden District." The Garden District, as is apparent by its name, is a place of well-manicured lawns and well-kept houses. Children can often be seen playing in front of their houses, which is an indication that the Garden District is a community that is well patrolled by local police officers. Most of the residents of the Garden District work in some kind of service-based profession, such as governmental industry, local education, state government, health care, or social service. Other communities have not been so fortunate.

One can spot the more unfortunate communities when driving through Salvation City because they are marked by older houses struggling to maintain their integrity against weather wear. Because these communities are older, many houses do not have adequate heating or plumbing. The infrastructure of these houses results in significant maintenance costs, including electrical, plumbing, and heating bills. When houses in these more unfortunate communities are viewed from the street, one can see problems with roofing and peeling siding that have been neglected for two or possibly three generations. There is some graffiti that marks the area as well. The town government has successfully turned away many attempts to establish places of ill repute such as strip clubs, dive bars, and pornographic establishments in these areas. The proliferation of bars has been of paramount concern because the fear of violence associated with alcohol has often sparked the concern of many community members.

Leaders in Salvation City, particularly those who have been in public office since the 1970s, realize that they have a lot of fallout to deal with. We spoke with Penny, a local civic leader in Salvation City. At the time of her interview, Penny was an elderly but attractive widow who was involved in many community efforts to improve the waning city. A bright, cheerful, and beautiful smile defined this woman, who was nearing seventy-four when we spoke to her at a downtown 1950s Art Deco diner that might be taken as a symbol of Salvation City's more

prosperous days. Unlike many diners in the city that start up and immediately close down, this diner had a long history kept alive by its proximity to a well-policed area.

Penny's father, who had passed away almost ten years before the
interview, was a local business leader and a bank manager. Penny's husband worked at a local factory to put himself through college and then
went on to a life in civil service. This gave Penny a unique awareness of
many of the problems that she had to deal with as a community leader:

> I can't solve all the problems. My interests lie in the structure
> of government. And I've seen that change drastically since 1943.
> But I have a humanitarian interest and I care about the children. I
> don't have a simple solution to the problems of the city's decline.
> But I would like to see it as a public place where people aren't
> called insensitive or bigoted.
>
> (Personal interview: Penny)

Penny spoke about hanging out at the pharmacy after high school, a common practice in the 1950s, and offered detailed accounts of the specific
type of business that once operated successfully within the boundaries of
Salvation City. She also recalled the importance of charity, as well as the
lively nightlife, in the city:

> During the 1950s, there were banquet halls, movie theaters, res-
> taurants and shops. The town was full of life. Stores were open
> late not only on Thursday night, but Friday nights as well. Post-
> WWII was really the glory days in Salvation City. We had three
> movie theaters and several clothing shops. The local university
> students would come down from Capitol City for the nightlife by
> bus, or they would hitchhike into the town, and people were good
> about giving them rides. We also had police and fireman's dances
> for charity and the benevolence society.

However, rumors of a large factory closing began to emerge during the
late 1950s. This turn of events might have marked the initial downturn of
Salvation City and its communities. Although the factory did not close
for many years, Salvation City's economy entered a slow and grueling

period of decline. Factories began to moderately downsize during the 1960s and shut down altogether during the 1970s. Although, according to many sources, Salvation City was always an entertainment hub, it was perhaps at this point that drug addiction and alcoholism came to be perceived as a problem that affected the community.

PATTERNS OF ADDICTION AND COMMUNITY DECLINE IN SALVATION CITY

Like many other American cities, the decline of community life in Salvation City can be indirectly linked to the crumbling citywide economy. As the major factory fell, so did residents perceptions' of quality of life. We interviewed Joshua, a recovering addict, who worked near an abandoned factory and shared an apartment with several older former factory workers who were expelled by their employer when the factory closed down. Under different circumstances, Joshua himself might have been a factory worker.

Today, the 34-year-old Joshua works a series of odd temporary jobs. He receives no medical or dental benefits for his work and has done almost every kind of task for money to survive in Salvation City's economy. He has mowed lawns, painted houses, and even worked directly for several social service agencies in a limited capacity.

> It was a shock when the factory finally closed, I knew it was a dying business, but there was a big sign on the outskirts of the town welcoming people to the town where the factory was. This was really a town that showed pride in the factory way. When they finally closed it was banner news in the local newspaper. Like Pearl Harbor...front page...the factory was moving and relocating to the south on short notice. Boom!
>
> (Personal interview: Joshua)

During the recession of the 1970s, the town's principal industries were outsourced. Perhaps because of the lack of appropriate employment opportunities, substance abuse became a major problem in Salvation

City. But, the town also has a long tradition of charity regarding substance abuse rehabilitation, as well as a history of problems with substance abuse in the area.

Substance use and abuse has always been a part of the culture of Salvation City. No one really knows when it first became so, but numerous legends and histories describe Salvation City as a primary hotspot for prohibition violations and, later, as a regional hub for the distribution of heroin. The problem was compounded during the prosperous years of the city by the active nightlife described by Penny. This problem has frustrated the town leadership for many years, but the problem still persists.

During the 1800s, Salvation City was targeted by temperance activists who sought to rid America of alcohol. The Women's Christian Temperance Movement was set up in the late 1800s, and history books from the beginning of the 20th century indicate that temperance resolutions were passed in Salvation City in the hope that temperance could be socially promoted. Salvation City itself was once the birthplace of a governmental report on "feeblemindedness" (an antiquated medical term for "severe mental deficiency") as a cause of crime (Bailey, 1919). It was commonly believed among intellectuals in Salvation City that feeblemindedness led to criminality. There is much to indicate that Salvation City was ahead of its time in promoting residential care for criminals or otherwise disabled people.

During the immigrant migration of the mid to late 19th century, business leaders in Salvation City began to show concern about alcohol addiction among immigrants. This rich tradition of charity is probably one of the primary factors that led to the establishment of halfway houses in Salvation City in the 1970s.

Once factories began to downsize and close, these halfway houses began to establish themselves as centers of debate in some communities. Because there was a lack of possible solutions to accommodate the growing problem with substance abuse in Salvation City, local authorities needed to do something about siting and placement of halfway houses.

SALVATION CITY'S HALFWAY HOUSES

The most likely places to be targeted as sites for halfway houses, as discussed in Chapter One, are disenfranchised communities who have very little power to resist placement. In addition to containing substance abuse residential treatment centers, Salvation City also has other criminal halfway houses and psychiatric halfway houses. Although it is possible that many temporary residences operate "under the radar," it is highly unlikely that they are in operation in the Garden District discussed earlier.

Penny was responsible for one of Salvation City's first efforts to maintain communities. She was instrumental in the foundation of one of the city's largest social programs:

> [...] and I'm sure you knew the development. It just grew and grew and grew. And it wasn't accepted in the community in the beginning. The problem for Salvation City is that there are just too many [halfway houses].
>
> (Personal interview: Penny)

Penny continued:

> While I don't have any objection. Personally I'm supportive of that. I see the value of halfway houses. The thing that makes me angry is that the state has allowed the private sector to run around town buying up houses and plunking halfway houses down in neighborhoods that are inappropriate. And that causes something called white flight and that's not fair. But houses in the neighboring town they all have buses they can bus people into town for the services that they need, and I get really angry about that. Whenever there is a public hearing, the Social Service Organization in Capital City will send their people in to protest. You know that really made people angry. Of course I fought the mayor and the City Council. They did nothing to protest the state, and they have that power! And I stood up in public and said so.

During the 1970s, Penny was instrumental in establishing the first local coordination between the government and community toward residential housing for substance abusers in Salvation City, but she showed a reluctance to accept the existence of "too many" halfway houses in Salvation City. Her concerns about "white flight" are completely valid. As a public official, she realized the importance of perceived safety within communities. Therefore, although her view of the halfway house in communities may appear somewhat paradoxical, it is based on legitimate concerns. These same concerns are those concerns about ethics that we continue to tackle throughout this book.

Despite the decline of communities in Salvation City, it has become the ideal place for a halfway house. It is an otherwise dark place where residential assistance is a beacon of light to those seeking change for the better. A place that used to be famous for its industry and associated opportunities, Salvation City can best be described as a waning town that has seen its better days.

SALVATION CITY'S HALFWAY HOUSE COMMUNITIES

Salvation City's decline is perhaps best demonstrated by the many boarded up and abandoned shops that decorate the halfway house district. Yet, if one were to look for an ideal location to set up a Value-Driven Recovery Oriented recovery community, the halfway house district of Salvation City would be near the top of the list.

There is an abundance of large, affordable multifamily houses. These houses are located within walking distance of most basic amenities. Two major grocery stores are located on Main Street. Convenience stores are scattered around town. Health care is available through local clinics and the Salvation City Hospital. The public library is centrally located. Although the closing of shops in the halfway house district brought immediate economic hardship to residents in that area, they were replaced by franchised shops and convenience stores that are further than a short walk from the more desirable middle-class and upper-class residential areas of the city.

Salvation City, in sum, is an attractive location for a significant cluster of halfway house programs geared toward drug addict or correctional transitional supervision. This chapter outlines the nature of some of Salvation City's programs and what the residents of Salvation City halfway houses go through in their daily life. Salvation City offers many advantages as a location for cost-effective, quality service.

The halfway house district of Salvation City contains various types of halfway houses. These houses, which include work-release houses, substance abuse houses, and mental health houses, are located within walking distance of many resources necessary for people in a transitional phase.

It is also important to note that the crime rate around the location of halfway houses in Salvation City is not much different than the crime rates of many cities across the United States. The private residences that border the district are not considered high-value houses. They are largely lower-middle class, with a small percentage of homes occupied by residents receiving governmental rent subsidies such as the Section 8 program.

By all other accounts, the halfway house district of Salvation City is an otherwise unremarkable area. Many people have found hope, recovery, and a better life in Salvation City's idyllic halfway house district. The area is an ethnically diverse area that offers a significant array of opportunities for people in transition. The halfway house zone is also located in a small taxing district that is an ideal location for many non-profit social services to operate in. There are several reasons for halfway houses to be located in Salvation City:

1. Residents of the homes often lack transportation. Walking to grocery stores, health care, restaurants, and various other services is possible for most able-bodied individuals.
2. ousing is less expensive than in neighboring communities. Nonprofit social service agencies wishing to build halfway houses or sober houses might be able to purchase and renovate buildings in Salvation City for a relative fraction of the cost.
3. The existence of a nearby hospital allows for easy access to health care.
4. There are many concerned, skilled, and dedicated professionals in the recovery field working in the region.
5. The low crime rates and nonexistence of gang activity, open-air drug markets, and prostitution in the area.
6. The absence of bars, strip clubs and nightclubs from the area.

RECOVERY IN SALVATION CITY

The primary goal of the Salvation City Department of Mental Health and Addiction Services is to ensure the provision of Value-Driven Recovery Oriented recovery community. Through its funding of programs, the government has assumed the role of social service provider. As such, it is the job of the government to provide services for populations that cannot take care of themselves. Although scholars in the Criminology field are in agreement that a high quality of service should be delivered, the reality of budgetary constraints that affect Salvation City does not always make this possible. Like most other local governments, the Salvation City Council has faced a recent governmental budget crisis. Tax revenues have decreased and calls for higher taxes are unpopular.

The Government Performance and Results Act (GPRA)—a body of legislation passed at the federal level during the Clinton administration—requires perfomance monitoring for both federal and state government–sponsored programs (Radin, 1998; Kravchuk & Chack, 1998). In accordance with the GPRA, governmental agencies are calling for the programs they fund to demonstrate success in rehabilitation along with financial accountability. Although there are some commissioned reports on the ability of halfway houses to effectively function, we provide several case studies from Salvation City that document the successes and failures of such programs with a greater deal of specificity.

CASE STUDY 1: LUIS FERNANDEZ

Luis Fernandez was born in 1978 in Puerto Rico. Before he was placed in a Salvation City halfway house, he traveled back and forth from Puerto Rico to the United States as a drug trafficker. After a prison term, Luis spent over six months in one of Salvation City's halfway houses. From an early age, Luis had trouble in school and dealt with drugs, mischief, and violence.

> I come from an environment with a lot of drugs, a lot of violence. For us, we never saw a way out and for us ... it was a way of life.

And what I started living with I started learning and what I started learning I started practicing. And what I started practicing, I became. And what I became had consequences in life. That's what happened to me. It's incredible to me that at an early age I started doing a lot of bad things that a normal eight-year-old kid don't do: I was a thief. I was a liar. I was a cheat. I was a liar. I was a fighter. You know what I mean?

(Personal interview: Luis)

Addiction to alcohol and drugs ran in Luis's family. When he was eleven years old, he was a fourth-grade dropout. Luis joked: "And I don't say this to brag because I'm not proud of it."

According to Luis's story, he did not drop out. Rather, school authorities kicked him out of fourth grade. Luis was nearly eleven years old when he got his first handgun and began to dabble with injecting narcotics.

The way I used to see it was they obligated me to, you know what? Forget about school and I'm going to survive in the jungle. What happened was while my brothers and sisters were in school, I was chillin' in the corner. I wasn't doin' stuff a normal 11-year-old kid would. I chose a life of crime. I was 11 years old and I already had a gun. I had a needle in my arm. It's incredible.

Like many Puerto Ricans, Luis came from a family that was very poor. His mother grew up with the title of "welfare mother" and his family survived off of food stamps. According to Luis, his mother tried very hard to keep him out of a life of crime, but in the end she could not help him.

She did the best she can, man. I chose to, now I understand that—to do a life of crime. By the age of 18 I had already broken every law. Name it. I had already broken every law... I was good in sports but I wasted my talent doing stuff I was not supposed to do. But I tell people you don't believe in miracles, well I do. You're seeing one.

Luis spent most of his youth moving from Ponce, Puerto Rico to the Bronx, New York, never having had a real home to speak of. He was arrested and placed in several different programs for juvenile offenders in the Bronx and Puerto Rico, and it is possible that the halfway house was his first stable abode other than prison. According to Luis, a stable home is very important among Puerto Ricans, who feel alienated in the United States. He spoke of a "geographic cure" for homesickness that is common in his culture. However, each time he moved, it was to a different area that he described as a "ghetto."

> My mother suggested that geographic cure they talk of: go back to Puerto Rico. And I used to love it because I could leave behind all that stuff, all that mess. Then back in Puerto Rico I found myself open to more of the bad stuff, more intelligent, and more experience. And then, once again, I go back to the Bronx and once again, each time I move it was the same thing: it was a ghetto. It was a barrio. It was a project. You know what I mean?

For Luis there seemed to be no way out. He admitted to believing that the American dream was to sell drugs and make money.

> And buy my house and buy my cars and be up and down and being a ghetto gangster. I pretended to be something that I never was. I wanted to be Billy the Kid. I wanted to be John Wayne, you name it. So what happened at an early age I started doing juvie time for robberies in little Chinatown and gas stations.

Although Luis did not consider himself a violent criminal, he admitted to participating in armed robberies—however, solely for financial reasons. At age twenty-three, Luis was picked up for selling drugs. At the time of his arrest, Luis was also armed.

Luis's life prior to his incarceration and subsequent stay at a Salvation City halfway house was filled with instability and tragedy:

> In 1980, my father was shot in the head by drug dealers. And let me tell you that my father abandoned me when I was small. I never had love for a stranger. So when I was growing up, people would ask me, are you capable of avenging the death of your father? I'd say no, man, know what I mean? Hell no! Then later

down the road they killed one of my best friend's brothers because they were trying to catch up with us. And then what really happened was I got involved. I got in shootouts and I got involved with people that were doing really bad things. I really believed all the good, the bad and the ugly. I tried to be a character that I never was.

Luis used to consider himself a "Robin Hood" figure in his local community, robbing from the "rich" and giving everything to the poor. Despite his own methods of moneymaking, he spoke contemptuously of drug dealers:

I always take care of my people in my neighborhood. I used to love going to war with drug dealers, the people that sold drugs. And they think that they are all that, they are superior to other people. They treat the people that use down here real low. I was against them always. I was never against those people that worked every day to make a living. I was in the ghetto with the people from the ghetto, with criminals. With people like me who did bad things. That was my war. So like I said, I was not considered the most dangerous. But I was considered the most troublemaking because my fighting, my behaviors, and my attitude. I was undisciplined. When I went to jail at thirteen years old and I was happy because I knew that sooner or later I was going to die at the hands of another punk on the streets.

Luis confessed that when he first went to a juvenile facility at age thirteen, his addiction was taking over. As a juvenile, he realized that getting into trouble at a young age was protected by the law.

The law was protecting me because I was a juvenile and I'd be under the custody of my mother and I would go back home and I would just laugh. I was doing it like real simple. I always had an excuse and always had a reason, always blaming.

Things changed for Luis when he turned seventeen and legal authorities started treating him as an adult. He was, however, expecting the transition to prison life and probably more ready for it than most people.

And when that happened I was a little short kid ready to go to the big pen with the big boys. At that time I was in Puerto Rico and I came out of juvenile and they told me as I was coming out that the next case I would get, I would be treated as an adult. I didn't care. I just knew that it was the biggest hit in my life.

Luis's first prison conviction came as an adult sentence of eight years in Puerto Rico. After his conviction, an epiphany came for Luis that he described as "life-saving."

They offered me twelve years and I still was happy. I was happy because DOC rescued my life. I went into the system (In Puerto Rico). Over there is crazy. I mean, they'll kill you over ten dollars. I mean, you pull a trick on somebody they're capable of taking your life. I got identified in the lineup and they gave me twenty years in jail. I still was happy. I counted that I had past my teens and now my twenties in jail. Man, I'll still be a baby when I come out. I'll still take over the world. I went to jail driven by false pride. I went to jail a baby, man. I went to jail not knowing how to write and read, real young. That's when I started learning how to respect people, how to communicate with people, how to be friends with people like the love that my mother had for me

Luis served nine years, eight months, and eighteen days in a Puerto Rican jail. Although his sentence was extended to twenty years due to infractions committed in the jail, the court took seven years off of his sentence and allowed ten days off for every month that he worked and studied. When he got out, he was anxious to keep the promises he had made to his mother. He moved to the United States to take up residence with his sister in Capitol City.

However, shortly upon Luis's return to Capitol City, he again found himself embedded in a life of crime. He explained that his return to crime was not so much for personal reasons, but to acquire proper medical attention for his mother who could not obtain such treatment in Puerto Rico.

When I got out, I made so many promises to my mother.... I got arrested for selling to an undercover cop. I got arrested because

> I had a pistol, I got arrested for trespassing, I got arrested for possession of drugs. My mother was suffering from diabetes. Over there [in Puerto Rico], the treatment is not as good as the United States of America, so my mother came in '92, and I came in '97. I went to New York City. I had to pick up some money. I had to pick up some drugs and I headed to Capitol City.

The court had mercy on Luis and sentenced him to three years in prison, followed by a stay at a halfway house for substance abusers in Salvation City. Although the traditional treatment program in a halfway home runs for only nine months, Luis was able to extend his stay for two years. During his interview, he was very critical of American prisons, claiming that he was involved in both gangs and drug selling while in prison

Luis referred to the program as wonderful, pointing out the importance to his current success of having a stable residence.

> In that wonderful program my journey begins. I tell people that I was in jail and I had the ability to use and abuse. When I was in the state pen I was always in trouble. I was a gang member. I was in the hole always. I was at war with other gang members, families. I came out of prison almost three years ago. But what still happened was I had reservations on me. I didn't want to use drugs but I still wanted to sell drugs and make money because I didn't have no skills. I never in my life had a job. I wanted that environment. I wanted to go to nightclubs; I wanted to be in the corner chillin'. I wanted to drive all kind of cars. Not knowing that I was making an appointment to go back to jail.

Like several other prisoners, Luis considers himself a very spiritual man. He rationalizes his situation as an act of God:

> I'm a true believer in Jesus. I believe in God. But what I believe was happening was that I was doing it my way. God has been good to me. I got shot in my leg. I got shot in the back of my neck. When I was in juvenile, I was going to take revenge. I escaped and two days later, I got in a wreck. But then I was a fugitive and when I opened my eyes in the hospital they were waiting for me.

> All those battles that I've been in, I believe that God was looking out for me. And what happened was that I got sentenced to do four years. I went to jail. I was happy.

Before his entry into the Salvation City halfway house program, Luis had been granted parole for a temporary period of time. During this time, he was ready to enter a life of crime once again. However, his mother's death undoubtedly affected his will to succeed in the halfway house program.

> I remember my mother touching my hand and saying "Luis, you are a wonderful man." And I had a gun on me, a nine millimeter automatic pistol and I had some drugs on me. And what I remember was I flushed the drugs down the toilet and I tried to flush the pistol but it was too big. So I flushed all my drugs away and then sooner or later, I was hopeless. I didn't know what to do with my life. I got approved parole and at that time I wanted to see the street. I was missing a couple of people. I wanted to get the people to give me an explanation on why they didn't help me out when I was sitting in the state pen. Why they left me for dead. But I still had these reservations.

In the halfway house, Luis was able to refocus his life, "find God," and have a chance to be treated for addiction and anger problems.

> Before the halfway house, I never in my life had a chance to do treatment, probation or parole, never. I was punished to do jail time. And that's incredible, man. Because I went through what I went through in my life for a reason, man. And I hear people and I tell people and I go to meetings and do a lot of twelve-step fellowship. And I hear people and they say, "hey, this happened to me" and I don't want to be one of them.

Luis was at first skeptical about the Salvation City recovery house program, but after his mother's death he was willing to take a chance and commit himself to recovery.

> So I gave myself a chance and started working on myself and a lot of stuff started happening. While I was there eight months,

I started going to school for my GED and now it's time to get a job, to move on. I got a choice to make a living and where I'm going to live. Or I can decide to go back to a life where I don't have no job, no education and sooner or later I'll go back to selling drugs in order to survive, to eat.

Luis is visible in Salvation City today. He no longer lives a life of crime and violence. Instead, he works at a legitimate job in a restaurant and can frequently be seen reaching out to other recovering addicts through a coalition for addiction recovery. He was the beneficiary of numerous programs, among them a recovery house that supported him as he made his attempt to get a job, save money, and avoid the potential relapse into significant substance use and the numerous problems that dominated his past.

In many cases, conventional wisdom would have dictated that society is best off giving up on people like Luis. However, he credits the support of the programs in Salvation City for having turned around a lifetime of problems.

For Luis, the recovery process was an active experience. In his work, Luis tries to put a positive face on recovery. Few addicts share their stories with the general public. Many people in addiction recovery follow twelve-step programs that stress anonymity. The medical model of recovery stresses confidentiality with medical records and diagnoses as well. Because there are few outspoken advocates sharing their stories of success in recovery homes, there are not many clear voices lobbying and articulating the positive experiences of those in recovery homes other than professionals that work in the treatment and recovery field. Luis is an exception.

Recovery homes are a public good that benefited Luis, but they also provide a substantial benefit to society as a whole. Luis is no longer acting out criminal behavior and perpetrating damage to society. He is no longer taking up space in the expensive and significantly overcrowded correctional institutions.

CASE STUDY 2: PAUL

Luis's story is that of a person who used the halfway house system in Salvation City to go from poverty and crime to a respectable life, but it is important to recognize that not all halfway house participants are sent there by coercion. Such is the case with Paul, a 45-year-old businessman who voluntarily admitted himself to a temporary residential facility for recovery in Salvation City.

> Like I say, I was driven to AA by circumstances, nothing other than circumstances. If I had been able to continue to carry on I would have. I just basically exhausted all the resources. I couldn't earn the money anymore, I couldn't run the game anymore. I couldn't make up any more excuses. It was simply, "OK, I'll go do something about my drinking because you [his wife] think I have a problem."
>
> (Personal interview: Paul)

At the time of his self-admittance to the halfway house, Paul was the owner of an auto repair shop that he struggled to maintain while having constant alcohol addiction problems. He reported that at the level at which he was drinking, he was not able to perform basic repairs on automobiles, falling asleep during brake repairs and forgetting to change lug nuts while performing wheel alignments.

Paul was a classic closeted alcoholic, whose wife, Debbie, did not know about his drinking. One day, while he was at work, his wife discovered his hidden stash of bottles.

> Debbie just went through the place and filled up a fifty-five gallon drum with Vodka bottles that were everywhere: behind the furnace, in the drawers, in the bedroom, in dirty rag bags. And when I actually saw that I was amazed. Those aren't all mine. Where did those all come from?

Upon his self-admittance to the residential program in Salvation City, Paul had many concerns about his business and his family. Residents of halfway houses who come from impoverished conditions do not usually experience such concerns.

> How will my family get by without me? And what about my business and all my customers? The reality was, of course, there

weren't any more customers and the family couldn't wait to get rid of me. And actually, once I was there I was happy to be there. Because I was out of the immediate fire zone, completely out of sight and out of mind. I mean, they fed you well, gave you stuff to do all day, encouraged you, they were hopeful.

After twenty-eight days in the recovery program, Paul started to clear up mentally and see the true picture. With the help of a trained substance abuse counselor, Paul began to get his life back in order. However, once the initial sobering-up process had occurred, Paul admitted that he was perhaps overconfident in his ability to return to the community and remain sober.

...the counselor I had said, "I don't think you should go right back home. I don't think it's a good idea. I don't think you have your sober feet on the ground yet. Let's see if I can go make arrangements at a more permanent residential treatment program. You can go and stay there."

Paul did not like his second temporary residence as much as he did his first 28-day inpatient stay. He complained that his life was more regulated in the second institution:

I didn't like it because you sort of lost freedom. I mean, you could come and go, but there were certain places that you had to be at certain times. And you would have to get up at seven o'clock or some ungodly hour. I said, "Why do I have to get up? I'm not going to a job." And if you didn't get up, the director of the place would come in and wake you up. I mean, she would come into your room and shout at you and make you get up and it was like structure into my sloppy, undisciplined, lazy life.

During his stay in the halfway house, Paul really did not think of himself as somebody who needed to get a job.

Well, it was considered a working halfway house but since I already had a job and the town of Coventry could put a lien on my house, I told the [halfway] house that I was self-employed and I was going to go back to the business once I got out of there. They went along with it because they were getting paid.

This made his residential stay there somewhat difficult. He had obvious concerns about his own auto repair shop and how he would get it running again once he got out. "I kind of resisted that. I can only say, looking back on it, it was good for me. I just couldn't do what I wanted."

Paul went on to explain the living structure at the halfway house. In addition to not being very happy with his highly regulated situation, Paul was also unhappy with being placed in a very small room with a roommate that he did not care for and in conditions that he considered unsanitary.

> That was another thing. You had to have a roommate. In the detox center, you had a room to yourself and it was all nice. The halfway house was like a giant step down, a ragged old place with all this dirty, filthy carpet. It's just a run-down sort of place. I had to have a roommate. You had to share a bath space. But I stayed there for three months nonetheless.

In the end, after a three-month stay, Paul said they "honorably discharged" him so that he could get back to the lifestyle that he was used to. Problems were building up at home, and there was a part of him that wanted to stay in the halfway house. However, he and the counselors that he worked with realized his need to return to reality.

> Because, really, I didn't want to go home and face the music. It was still better than some sort of abstract memory of "things aren't going too good. The bank is still trying to foreclose." Debbie would show up from time to time across the street at McDonald's and she would just be in a tizzy. I mean, "What are we going to do?" and all that. I'd tell her, "Don't let it disturb your serenity because it will all work out in some magical mystical way." There were times when she couldn't stand it.

Paul admitted that his stays in both the detoxification clinic and the halfway house had negative effects on his relationship with his wife. But, he indicated that the long-term situation with his own home life became better overall, largely due to his experience with rehabilitation and temporary housing.

> So overall, I'd have to say that both of them were good experi-
> ences though I didn't like it at the time. Like so much of my life,
> I don't know what's good for me and that's still true. And I met
> my [A.A.] sponsor that I still have today because outsiders would
> come to meetings, thank God. It's better than the blind leading the
> blind, a room full of people with 30 days collective sobriety try-
> ing to figure out what to do next.

Although Paul reaped the benefits of living in the halfway house, he
admitted to not returning once he was free of its constraints: "I didn't
really go back much. I didn't support the meeting much once I got back
to home."

Paul credited most of his success to the successful 12-step program
that he became involved in while residing in the halfway house. He
mostly claimed that residential housing took away his ability to lead a
parallel life in which he was trying to hide his alcoholism. The halfway
house gave him focus and allowed him time to reassess his priorities, as
well as meet people who had been through similar situations.

> We used to sit, Thursday nights it was relapse prevention and the
> guy [counselor] was very candid about it. He would stand up at
> this board and he would say things like one-tenth of one percent
> of you have a snowball's chance of staying sober for the next
> five minutes and all of us would groan. But the statistics that he
> quoted, I'm sure, were accurate. They were just trying to drive the
> point home. It really takes effort and it takes a certain amount of
> soul searching. It was just stuff that you had to do. They made you
> go to a meeting every single day. And if you didn't have a car you
> just walked. That was mandatory.

Again, we attribute a lot of Paul's recovery to the unique circumstances that surround Salvation City's halfway house district. However,
we were a bit surprised when Paul revealed that he had not made any real
connections with the people in the halfway house program with him:

> I didn't make any friends there. I was actually a little uncomfort-
> able there because actually it was kind of a crazy place, a crazy

place. A lot of the residents worked at a local landscaper service because that was the kind of job they could get. You know, you go down to that landscaping and work out in the sun all day for minimum wage. They would hoot and holler and they were a very boisterous group. I didn't really feel at ease when I was around them.

Paul, a white male from a suburban environment, admitted to feeling uncomfortable with many of the people he shared the halfway house with:

It kind of spooked me because there were a lot of streetwise tough, a lot of blacks and Hispanics. I was really out of my element around these guys. I didn't know how to have a conversation with them. I couldn't understand their language for the most part. You know the street talk. And I felt really like I had been thrown into the bowels of Hell.

Paul today

Some halfway houses' programs have become dumping grounds for the poor, but in Paul's case we see a case where a program was actually successful because a participant had some social capital to begin with. Paul was extremely motivated by the halfway house program because he wanted his house back. He wanted his family back. He wanted to get back to his stable and successful life. Fortunately, many of his old clients were pleased that he sobered up and business soon got back to normal for Paul.

One of the trucking companies that I contracted for in Capitol City. They were real supportive of me. The president of the place was just a real compassionate guy, I guess. I went to see him when I got home and told him I was trying to reconstruct my life and my business, and he thought I looked great and whatever and even he said the same thing, because I used to go over and work and figured "as long as you have the Hall's Mentholiptous cough drops nobody knows."

Paul's mention of cough drops was a reference to an earlier time in his life when he used them to conceal the alcohol on his breath. When interviewed, Paul found it alarming that he had previously been driving and operating machinery in his inebriated condition. One of the things that the halfway house program helped him to realize was that he was doing a poor job of covering up his double life "I thought they had no idea, of course, there were other tell-tale signs like slurred speech and I was stumbling. But I was pretty well convinced that I had them all bamboozled."

Paul told us that one of the good things about the halfway house program was that it gave residents questions and answers to think about, rather than "just rooms." They did introduce clients to a solution, according to Paul.

When asked about the integrity of the home program that he had resided in, Paul indicated that there were some strict rules. The program had integrity. The program had integrity and a large part of the success he has experienced since his release from the program was a result of the strict discipline used within the program. When asked if he had witnessed drug abuse in the halfway house, Paul indicated that he had not, but that there were several other reasons people were thrown out:

> There were people that got thrown out. I don't know about relapse, but there were people who were thrown out for just not sticking to the rules. They were really firm about that; you had to be back at the house, no excuses. It doesn't matter if a car broke down or if you called, too bad. There were people who got discharged for that, which seems sort of unfair. But there was no real loss for clients. I mean no shortage of clients. When one got booted out there was already one on the waiting list ready to come in.

Paul's final quote to us was meaningful and inspirational: "Everything looks different in the sober light of day. It looks different after a certain amount of years too."

CASE STUDY 3: SONNY

Sonny, forty-two years old, is the son of an influential educator in a small town on the outskirts of Salvation City. He recalled his hometown as a place that had hometown appeal, but little else to do besides visit mom-and-pop shops. As a kid, Sonny was very involved with athletic activity. He spoke of a park where he would play ball as a youth.

> The town had that. I mean, the Little League had the same sponsors every year, the same businesses. They were hanging in there, I guess. There were two clothing stores in the town I grew up in, they were lovely little places.
>
>   (Personal interview: Sonny)

Sonny's family grew up next to a family that was involved in the local factory at an executive level. He described his hometown as very stable and peaceful.

> One thing about the area that I do think has changed. I look back at the area as much more homogeneous. The income brackets were scrunched together. It wasn't a real affluent community. It was middle class. I wasn't aware of people having a ton of money but I also wasn't aware of poverty.

Unlike Luis, Sonny grew up with a stable home, stable childhood family situation and in a stable neighborhood. In many ways his story parallels that of Paul: "Growing up, I don't remember any crime, I don't remember seeing any drugs, but then again, generally we weren't exposed to it until the late sixties or early seventies and that's when it became apparent."

However, Sonny confessed that local drug use in his hometown area was well known by residents of Salvation City: "And the kids that I knew from Salvation City, when they thought about the kids from the outskirts, it was like, oh, pot smokers. I went to a high school where, like, everybody said 'they smoke pot.'"

Still, Sonny did not remember any violent crime from his hometown.

> Salvation City was certainly a bigger town than where I was living, but there was no fear factor [of crime] as a kid. I could walk down there as a kid eight or nine years old. Even in the sixties there was recognition that there was a Puerto Rican population. Even before then, Salvation City was known for having a Puerto Rican population. But I can tell you that was all part of the sixties; be it racism, be it segregation that the contact was very minimal.

I went to the public school system just outside Salvation City. It was 98 percent white. My remembrances of Salvation City as a young guy were great. But that was the sixties, mom and apple pie. I wasn't aware of any crime. Didn't see it, didn't read about it.

Sonny attributed a great deal of his problems to the fact that he grew up during the 1970s when drug use was in vogue and the restrictions regarding selling alcohol to minors were not heavily enforced. He stated:

I started drinking around school. For us, it was these house parties. If you wanted to get booze there was this package store with a little old lady who couldn't see and she'd ask you if you were eighteen and you'd nod yes. Or you'd ask a college student to buy some for you.

Sonny also admits that there were other package stores from which he was able to obtain liquor at an early age. "You could buy all over four or five package stores—didn't have to go to just one, also [...] high school had some eighteen-year-olds who could buy for you."

Sonny also said that there were more liberal school regulations in the 1970s that allowed him opportunities to drink and get involved in drugs:

My senior year, you could sign yourself out of school. Every Wednesday was a half day, and that would consist of getting beer and driving around drinking. I remember putting beer in my locker. I remember a teacher smoking pot but it wasn't sexually permissive and there were mostly intact families.

Sonny started smoking pot in high school and then began experimenting with heavier drugs, such as various pills, as he progressed.

Pot was readily available, and when I think about it, in high school it was the only drug around. The group that I hung around with had no interest in that heroin or LSD. But it was common to see somebody at a party who was tripping. Heroin I never saw. I knew it was there and I had a roundabout experience with it.

One of my good friends as a kid was a year or two older than me, a good family. Here is somebody from my neighborhood, white, middle-class, who got involved at a young age. It was just part of the area and time period, I guess."

At seventeen, he got into a tragic car accident that piqued community interest in teen drinking. However, he feels that he was not an alcoholic or addict at the time:

For me, I was kind of a weekend drinker. I wasn't one of those people, I know some people say I tried it and it was nirvana. The first time I got drunk, I said, "This is horrible and I'll never do it again." The DUI brought me in.

When he considered the drinking he did as a youth, Sonny was confused as to why this was his first DUI. He really did not consider himself an alcoholic, but found a great deal of appeal in the Alcoholics Anonymous program.

It was mandated that Sonny go through a local halfway house on an outpatient basis for alcohol addiction counseling and treatment. His choice to remain a member of Alcoholics Anonymous after the court-sanctioned diversion for his DUI was not mandated by the court, but came from his own positive experiences with rehabilitation.

Although it is unusual to see a seventeen-year-old show such a strong commitment to the Alcoholics Anonymous program, it is notable that Sonny, at age seventeen, had gone through almost 120 meetings in sixty days. Sonny said that he really enjoyed the program because of the feelings of family that he achieved in his interactions with the group. He was also required by the court to attend a DUI school along with his outpatient treatment.

I enjoyed the heck out of it [DUI school]. There were twelve of us in there, I think I was the only one who was in AA. We had an assignment to talk about alcohol in some way. I took the AA model. I went to 120 meetings in sixty days.

After he turned nineteen, Sonny ended his attendance at AA meetings and decided to pursue a career. He followed in his father's footsteps and became a high school coach, although he found the career unappealing because the leap to college coaching eluded him.

During the 1980s, Sonny quit his job as a local coach to open a small business. Although it was not lucrative, Sonny was able to make a steady income. As his life became more stable, he fell in love, got married, and became a father and an upstanding member of the community. Sonny lived in a relatively anonymous fashion, with no outstanding problems or financial difficulties, until he went back to becoming a casual drinker.

He used his own self-discipline to stop drinking again for about three years. "I stopped in late eighties, early nineties, for three years on my own." He attributed a large part of his ability to quit to the methods that he learned during his outpatient stay and subsequent recovery.

During the early 1990s, Sonny's life began to crumble once more. Sonny got a pained look on his face when we asked him to tell us about the details of his divorce and subsequent failure to get custody of his children. However, we assumed by the tone in his voice that Sonny was simply one of the many Americans who became another divorce statistic. There was no dramatic event that started his divorce, just a matter of irreconcilable differences between him and his wife. He was not drinking problematically at the time of his divorce or addicted to pills. In fact, Sonny's divorce was "just another divorce."

During his divorce, Sonny began to drink again. And when he went back to drinking, he drank heavily. Sonny, trying to maintain his business while secretly drinking at home, was able to maintain face in the community. One night, while drinking in the privacy of his own home, he blacked out. When he awoke, he found himself in need of a familiar place. Shortly after, Sonny was back in the same outpatient halfway house program that he was in when he was seventeen years old and sanctioned by the courts.

Two years and eight months sober at the time of this interview, Sonny told us that it was "a sign." He realized that there were assets in the community that he was not taking advantage of because of his attempt to hide his alcohol problems. He had forgotten about the home and was too embarrassed to return to AA.

After his brief readmittance to the halfway house outpatient program, he rejoined AA and to this day remains a productive member of the community. Although Sonny still struggles with his divorce, he knows that alcohol is not the answer to his problems, something that he attributes to his brief outpatient experience with the halfway house.

CASE STUDY 4: JANE

Jane, former resident of several temporary and foster homes, child of a single parent, and aged twenty-four at the time of her interview, sat outside a temporary housing facility in Salvation City. She sat on a bench between some magnolia trees in full bloom. Her eyes were blue and sad and revealed that there was a great deal of scarring underlying her otherwise cherubic face. Jane's childhood was probably to blame for most of her problems. When she was living with her mother, she started dealing drugs because her mother charged her rent. At age eleven, she was diagnosed with mental illness: "I started diagnosis at age eleven or twelve, at least sixth grade—schizophrenia, psychotic, borderline. I certainly had my fair share of acting out in hospitals but I didn't care. I was already locked up." (Personal interview: Jane)

When using the term "locked up," Jane referred to her foster family, which she had a personal distaste for:

> These people adopted me. My father's half brother and his wife. [...] These major Republicans and they took me in when I was about thirteen. The drug thing went OK. It was like, don't do drugs and I'd say OK and pop acid at the dinner table. And they would say isn't it nice that you're sober.

Because her foster parents suspected her affections toward another girl, they made her see a psychologist. "They told the doctor I was using and suicidal; actually, I was quite happy. I had three trips to separate psychiatric institutions because of them."

At age fifteen, Jane was again committed to a psychiatric institution when she overdosed on prescription medication. "I think by the time

I was fifteen, I was on fifteen different classes of narcotics," she joked. "I remember, I would go up to the local pizza parlor and buy French fries and snort ketamine."

When Jane was first admitted to the psychiatric institution, the doctors' immediate reaction was to place her on several medications for her known psychiatric conditions: "They did put me on everything in the book. If that didn't work, they put me on something worse. They had me on Thorazine, even."

Jane complained that her experience with the hospital was unpleasant and not conducive to healing:

> [...] the worst thing I remember about the psychiatric hospital was you overdose, then they bring you to the hospital, then they pump your stomach. At the hospital, I slept on the floor because they didn't have a bed. It wasn't bad, but the next day they bombard you. I mean, I just tried to wreck my body, and it's like ninety-nine people come up to you and they give you this insane several hundred question bubble thing and it's like: Do you, like, do you like sports? How often did you try to commit suicide? Are you blonde?

Jane even told us a story of an abusive doctor that she had an encounter with during her stay in the psychiatric hospital:

> The head of the psychiatric hospital drugged me up all the time. He was a real fruitcake [...] and he'd be like, if you don't take your medication I'm going to send you back to the hospital. I mean, he'd take me off cocaine and put me on Serentil [an anti-psychotic used in the treatment of schizophrenic patients], which was like smoking an ounce of weed or something. Have you ever seen some of the stuff they put these kids on? It's ridiculous.

Jane also said that there were some staff members that seemed to act with integrity, but she felt betrayed by some of them:

> Some people would come in staring at their clipboard and they'd look anywhere but anywhere you were looking. Or moronic phrases,

there was one lady who said wowie zowie all the time. It was like "lady, I'm not four, why are you wowie zowieing me all the time?"

After her experience with the overdose and subsequent institutionalization, Jane moved on to a new school, hoping to leave her past behind. But, she found out later that a hospital administrator had sent an unfavorable review of her to her new school:

> I got interviewed by a couple doctors and this woman came by, and when you see a comforting face, you appreciate it. And she wrote a very long report that was sent on to my next school that I was a manipulative person. I was really hurt and I didn't find out about it until about a year later. I mean, God, I was being nice.

After dropping out of high school at age nineteen, Jane experienced another overdose. Again she wound up in a psychiatric hospital and found the conditions there most unfavorable to her recovery:

> They put everyone together, the schizophrenics and the drug people and it's like jail where you come out worse than you were before. There were girls who were depressed and suicidal because they were abused by step-fathers or groups or whatever. And their stance on that—those hospitals was "it's not your problem—don't let it affect you." Everything was about the blue padded room. Because you are told to and that's your problem.

Defiant, and in despair, Jane began to act out during her stay at the psychiatric institution:

> One day I was caring about a girl and they would say: "that's not your role" [this is key because it casts in sharp relief how patient roles in an institution stress lack of concern about others, whereas halfway house environments create an atmosphere of distributed responsibility for other residents]. One day I guy told me to go back to my room and I told him no and if he didn't leave me alone, I would kick his knees in and he didn't believe me so I did it. It took six people to restrain me.

Jane also reported that the psychiatric hospital had a solitary confinement area for people caught breaking the rules:

> I got put in solitary confinement for twenty-four hours for smoking a cigarette. There are certain points when you are pushed too far and anybody would react. But that doesn't mean you are psychotic. I mean, considering all the stuff I'd been putting in my body, it's not very nice for them to take my cigarettes away too.

Jane described the drug and alcohol detoxification experience as being very painful: "Being a junkie in rehab is the worst thing in the world for the first two weeks. The first week of detox—you just hate everything—you want to crawl out of your skin."

When asked about the catalyst that motivated her to get her act together, Jane mentioned the story of a girl that she grew up with who overdosed on the same prescription medications she was taking. After that, she stated:

> I started to care about others more than myself. I think the thing that keeps me up at night is I watched so many people die. At some time I started latching on to other people until I could do it for myself, when you're in a relationship and you're going into rehab and you get into that real righteous phase for a few months.

Jane credited no small part of her recovery to her stay in a halfway house upon her release from psychiatric commitment at age nineteen. She attributed much of this to Gilberto, who was her instructor and affiliated with the halfway house at which she was staying.

> There was one very nice guy, Gilberto. His father was wealthy and contributed to building the local church. Gil was also a recovering alcoholic whose drinking got so bad that his wife left him. He had a Masters in English lit and got an MSW when he was younger.

Jane's experience with Gil was highly unconventional, considering the prescribed formal nature of the client/social worker relationship:

"The first time I met him he was building a seat or bench between the trees outside his office."

Jane was referred to Gilberto and his program after she overdosed. Most of her visits with him were highly unconventional:

> It was like what's wrong with you—like there's nothing wrong—what right did I have to be there? And most of my visits with him were rides on his motorcycle. I don't know if he ever charged my insurance. I must have seen him three times a week sometimes.

Gilberto was not a conventional social worker by any means. The way that his halfway house program was run was highly exceptional. His visits with patients often involved sporting activities or leisurely activities to get their mind off of drugs or alcohol. He was a charismatic personality and somewhat of a hero in Salvation City. Although many in the social work community would frown on his unorthodox methods, they seemed to work for Gilberto's clients; and since most of his work was charitable and with perceived societal outcasts, no one aggressively disputed his relationships with his clients.

Gilberto built two successful halfway houses in Salvation City, but died an untimely death at age fifty. Only an automobile accident limited the impact that Gilberto had on the community. However, his legacy was people like Jane, who remember him fondly and attribute a life of sobriety to his influence.

When we asked about Gilberto's contribution to her life and what he taught her, Jane answered with the following:

> That there was nothing more wrong with me than anybody else that came to see him. At that time I had been called weird and strange and freak and so many things for so long. And that's what I saw myself as because that's how everybody else saw me. I was defined by everybody around me, not by the person I wanted to be. I always wanted so much. When I was a little kid, I was like two steps ahead of my class, I was always, everything, the classic perfectionist child. But it didn't change anything. It didn't make my mother stop drinking or being a fruitcake. So by the time that

> I saw Gil, I had gotten to that point where I tried to stop trying to impress people and got to that point where it hurt so much that I started hurting myself—whatever form that took.

According to Jane, in sessions with Gilberto, the focus was not on analyzing her or giving her a diagnosis. "It was like, what do you want to do today? You want to get a coffee, let's go get a coffee or you want to go for a ride, let's go for a ride."

Jane successfully rehabilitated at one of Gil's halfway houses and continued to attend AA meetings on the premises after release. When asked if she returned after her three-month stay to speak with Gil, she said:

> I wanted to talk to him and tell him how good I was doing, but he just smiled and he knew. I think he just taught me that he was there and that was weird because there were so many people who said if you need help, come to me. And when you'd come to them, they'd just throw it back in your face. They would either punish you for coming for help or they'd hold it over your head or turn you into a charity case. There were always strings attached to help. Gil didn't have any strings attached. He got nothing from me. Even if he did, it was nothing compared to saving my life. He was just a real human being.

When asked about her personal recovery experience at the halfway houses and what residential housing did for her, she continued to allude to Gilberto's therapy as the most important part of her stay. However, it is likely that the halfway house environment provided her with her first stable home, even though she did not become as attached to the residents as she did to her counselor: "Now, I'm so out of recovery that people don't remember I was ever there. A lot of them were nice, but you could see they were protecting themselves by not feeling."

When we last spoke to Jane, she was a mother, engaged to be married to the father of her child, and enrolled at a regional university. As the three cases reported before her own (Luis, Paul, and Sonny), Jane's story projects a positive outcome by way of affiliation with a residential program in Salvation City.

It is telling that in the psychiatric hospital, Jane was not told to care about other patients but to mind her own business. In the halfway house, Jane was told the opposite: to care about the people she resided with and help them. It is obvious that the halfway house was an important part of Jane's current success. Although she continues to struggle with sobriety, she is fully aware that there are alternatives and is secure in her new life and identity.

CASE STUDY 5: BERNARD

Bernard, a 52-year-old advertising executive who is married with two children, drinks every day. However, his face still looks young, showing none of the signs typically associated with alcoholism. He prefers mixed drinks and admits to "turbocharging" (Personal interview: Bernard) his drinking on a daily basis with Vicodin. He obtains his Vicodin illegally and claims he does not have the time to "deal with doctors" because of his career. He acknowledges his problem with alcohol and drug addiction openly and says that it is something that he can live with as long as it does not affect his performance at work or his duties to his children.

Bernard has been down the road of recovery before, taking drugs on and off for several years. He claimed that his abuse problem began in high school with the recreational use of marijuana.

Bernard's high school story is that of many kids who start with alcohol and move on to marijuana and other drugs. In addition, Bernard, who had been playing drums since age thirteen, began hanging out with musicians at age fourteen or fifteen. "I played in a rock band when I was real young. I was in an environment where drugs were readily available. All I had to do was go to practice and somebody would light one up." In college, he continued on the path to try "[...] every drug available in college including cocaine, LSD, ecstasy, psychedelic mushrooms, and opium."

Bernard started college at a very young age (seventeen). He claimed that he was very impressionable and wanted to be friends with a lot of people. He joined a fraternity and soon found out that drugs were common among his new peer group. "College wasn't that much different from being in a band because when you are in the dorm room and everybody knows you're a head, people will start walking into your room and just do drugs."

Bernard's parents paid for college until he was nineteen and had his first episode with alcoholism, which involved a drunken fight with several members of his fraternity over a girl.

> Her name was Susan and she was much older, like twenty-four or so. I thought she was cheating on me with my frat brother. So I went out to a bar with a girl and got so drunk that I don't remember what happened […] but I woke up in the hospital and heard that I tried to fight an entire fraternity.

Bernard almost lost his vision in his left eye: "[…] my head was swollen like a grapefruit." There were no legal repercussions from Bernard's incident. However, soon after this incident, he found himself out of college due to other circumstances. After two years of college partying, Bernard was placed on academic probation. His parents withdrew financial support and he had to get a job.

> All my parents did was withdraw their financial support. They did not send me to a program because they thought I had just one episode and that was not going to be a permanent thing. They said I needed to get help, but they didn't do anything about it. Of course, I would've hated this anyway.

To stay sober, Bernard admitted that he had to use his own willpower. He began working at a local department store. He says he was trying to become "clean" after his incident. However, after about six months, he decided to make some extra money teaching drum lessons.

> I was supposed to be teaching at about ten bucks an hour, which was a fair price for back then. About one or two of the kids I taught would never have any money to pay me, but they always had weed. Looking back, I guess there was some kind of subconscious urge to keep doing drugs that led me back to music.

I mean, it really didn't bother me that they couldn't come up with money.

Eventually, Bernard was able to go back to college on money he had put away from working at the department store. Bernard's life of music eventually led to playing with several popular local bands, but he eventually quit because there was no money in it: "I decided to get out of music and go back to college, but I would still keep stocked up with weed from my old music buddies." Bernard decided to pursue a degree in business. While he was enrolled in college, he interviewed with a local advertising executive who gave him a job as an errand boy. He became highly influenced by his boss, Steve, who was also an alcoholic and drug user:

> I eventually enrolled for my MBA. I wanted to be in advertising because I envied the life that my mentors at the advertising agency had. I was really jazzed when Steve asked me to get him some weed and then coke. We got high together and he told me that all the other advertising executives did drugs.

According to Bernard, the fact that his bosses were able to live what he perceived as a "rock-and-roll lifestyle" made him more resolute in earning his MBA. Bernard also found out that many of the other graduate students either drank in binges to relieve tension or used drugs themselves. Whereas previously he had been a mediocre student, Bernard found himself at the top of his class in the MBA program despite his drug use and alcohol abuse.

> I successfully completed my MBA in 1988 and went right to work as a pitch man for a large company in advertising. I'm not going to tell you which one, because there's probably some people that still remember the scandals I was involved in. But I will tell you about the nature of my job, which was basically to sell advertising ideas to regional stores.

As was the pattern with most of Bernard's life, he seemed to attract "fellow stoners." He soon found himself among many peers who likewise used drugs and alcohol regularly. He was very successful in his early career, landing many accounts in his late twenties and early thirties.

> I think I was so young and boisterous that I came across as a real stoner. And I was a real stoner and would eat up pills like an anteater eats up ants. There was hardly any need to lead a double life, as most of my peers at the advertising agency were so similar.

By the time Bernard was thirty, he had attained tremendous financial success. He drove a $30,000 sports car and was paying a mortgage on a five-bedroom house. However, tragedy struck when Bernard was thirty-two and he became embroiled in a scandal involving a female intern employed at the advertising agency.

Bernard's romantic entanglement with the intern became complicated when her boyfriend found out—her boyfriend who was unemployed, very possessive, and very jealous that his girlfriend was succeeding in life. According to Bernard, her boyfriend

> [...] didn't like the idea of her talking to me and he reported us both. She happened to have a bunch of pills on her at the time, we both wound up getting arrested by the local cops. It made the local newspaper.

To avoid any further disgrace, Bernard had to resign from his position and take a leave of absence. In order to have the prosecutor divert charges, his lawyer instructed him to go into a rehabilitation program:

> My father had passed on but my mother was there, and she cared about me at the time. She wanted me to do a three-month inpatient stay, but my lawyer pointed out that since it was my first offense all I would need to do was enroll as an outpatient. Looking back, I see that I was a drug addict and an alcoholic. I should have listened to my mother, but I was too anxious to get back to work. I mean, you don't go to school for ten years and then spend time fiddling around in a nut hatch trying to evaluate yourself.

Bernard lamented that after the scandal, all of his colleagues at the advertising agency turned their back on him. He claimed that even the ones that did drugs with him, or got him to be a middleman, did not come to see him after his arrest. The bank eventually foreclosed on his home, although he was able to keep his sports car.

For five months after his incident, Bernard attended mandatory group sessions and found himself with a new job at another advertising agency in another state. With the charges dropped by the prosecutor, he hoped that his past would not shadow him. Bernard felt that alcohol was not a problem, only drugs, and continued to drink, though in moderation, during that time. However, due to problems with back pain, Bernard felt forced to ask his doctor for prescription medication:

> Because I had left behind all of my known drug connections and was probably still an addict, I started drinking so heavily that I gained about forty pounds. I went from 180 to 220. I kept having problems sleeping at night from back pain. I went to the doctor and told him and he gave me a prescription for Vicodin, which was ironic because it was the same stuff that I was busted with in the first place. With this prescription, I was able to cut my drinking down tremendously and began to lose weight again. And for a while, I was alcohol-free, though I took medication. It was an unusual time for me because somebody offered me weed and I turned it down. So pretty much for three or four years, the medication was all I was on.

Bernard's is a case where substance abuse in moderation lasted a few years without causing significant life problems. During this time, Bernard was able to get married, have two children, and hold down a job. As is the case with most drug abusers, Bernard eventually relapsed.

> I was getting on my feet with a permanent job and then one night I get a call from an uncle telling me that my mom's house burnt down. People don't know what it's like to have all your childhood memories destroyed. My mother was homeless and she had to move in with my aunt. I felt guilty because here I was, nearly forty years old and I couldn't take care of my elderly mother. Coming from my family, this was hard because my uncles took care of their parents.

It was at this point when Bernard returned to "turbocharging" his prescription pills with mixed drinks. He also began to seek out other drugs during this time, knowing from past experience where to get them:

> And so knowing the things that I knew in the past, I started hang-
> ing out in local music clubs and it wasn't long that I had access to
> all the things that I had when I was in my wild days. When I went
> back to the drugs, my work performance got sloppy.

Bernard started taking the Vicodin that was prescribed for him at night while getting other drugs off the street. His career in advertising continued, but became complicated at around age forty-two when his job performance and profits greatly dropped off. "I don't know who I think I was fooling, but I think that my colleagues could tell that I had addiction problems. Advertising executives toe the line nowadays, not like the ones that mentored me."

According to Bernard, he was showing up late for meetings every day "[…] and I think my clients were starting to recognize that my slurred speech was more than a speech impediment. One day I fell asleep at my desk at work. My boss called me into his office later and told me that I had to pack my stuff up and go." At age forty-two, Bernard had to start all over again and find a new career, although this time the specter of his past would not haunt him so much. "I guess somewhere in the back of my mind I was hoping for mercy or understanding, but rumors abounded […] watercooler gossip […] I found myself in a situation where I was jobless again."

Bernard committed himself to a halfway house in Salvation City after losing his second job. After a drug and alcoholic detoxification program, and a ninety-day stay in a halfway house, he was able to move on to another position. "Sure, I had had my share of incidents, but my resume looked pretty good. I had a lot of experience in advertising. It's almost funny that most of that experience came when I was loaded."

While Bernard was in the halfway house, he was able to stay clean without temptation. He attributed his success to strict regulation in the presence of the staff and other residents who genuinely wanted to help him:

> It was weird because I didn't crave anything in the time I was
> there. I was sharing a room with a former tugboat captain

[Dave] who had lost his license. I knew that as tugboat captain he probably made a lot more money than me. I wasn't the only person making money with a respectable job who had fallen far. I think most of all I was gathering myself in the halfway house. Collecting my thoughts about my mother, family, and my life situation.

Bernard continued: "My doctor, who helped admit me, said it would be hard, and took me off of my Vicodin after I finished the home."

But Bernard's stay in the halfway house was not a success, even though he could relate to some of his peers in treatment. It is possible that Bernard never truly finished the halfway house program, as he said earlier.

Bernard's failed halfway house stay occurred due to several reasons. He recalls age being a problem and an obsession with getting "back to work" reemerging during his last few weeks:

In my profession, you just can't be out of work for too long, or people will raise questions. I think that it was more important to me to get back to work than it was to stay sober. I think in the end, even my counselors recognized that I was going to relapse [...] so did I.

After putting in several applications, Bernard assumed he was recovered about ten years ago. His first year at his new position kept him so busy that he did not have time to drink or do drugs.

I felt like I had a lot to prove, so I started pulling all nighters. I smoked about three packs of cigarettes at night and worked on ad campaign pitches all night long. After the first year, though, my back started to kill me.

Bernard got a running start at his new position, landed several clients, and started making more money than he ever had. However, after things were going well again for him, he started drinking and perceived a need for painkillers again:

My back started hurting again and I began to drink heavily again. I started frequenting music stores again and made a solid connection.

I also had a friend at the time who suffered from hip problems and couldn't take his Vicodin because he claimed it hurt his stomach. He used to give them to me, but I'd drop a C-note on him once in a while.

Today Bernard is an active alcoholic and addict. His story is one of halfway house failure. He continues to drink on a daily basis. As we spoke about his story, he appeared to be truly torn about his next step.

CASE STUDY 6: SEAN

Sean, a distinguished looking 45-year-old gentleman, sat behind a desk and spoke to us about his recovery at a halfway house. Sean, a human resource administrator, grew up in the heart of Salvation City, where he went to a local Catholic school. Sean's is a story of hope and addiction recovery maintenance of which he was proud to speak. When we spoke, he was celebrating twenty-three years of sobriety.

I remember my first beer goes back to when I was three, maybe four years old with my grandfather and my father. We went to church, then we went to my grandparents' for lunch. Since I was a boy, I went with the men outside while the ladies stayed inside and cooked and gossiped together.

Sean also recounted that his experience in the Boy Scouts was slightly different than what the average boy experiences: "While I didn't drink all that often, I remember drinking as a Boy Scout on campouts."

Sean guessed that he started drinking alcohol regularly at around age twelve. At fourteen, when he discovered marijuana, he really enjoyed getting high and drinking. Sean said that he did not drink frequently. Instead, his pattern was binge drinking that led to episodes of alcoholism that often resulted in trouble:

I was a good kid, I was not looking for trouble […] I wasn't looking for a fight or to bother anybody and didn't want anybody to bother me […] but I just didn't know when to stop some time.

Sean talked about an incident that occurred when he was twelve years old and coming home from his sister's birthday party.

> There was a keg of beer and I didn't know anybody at the party. They were all teenagers there, and I befriended one of my sister's friend's younger brothers and we drank together all that night. The other teenagers thought it was cute and funny to see some twelve-year-olds drinking.

Sean admitted that he enjoyed being drunk. Sean, who by his own admission was shy as a youth, also liked "teenage" parties, so he accepted drinking as part of his lifestyle at an early age.

Later in his life, as Sean's marijuana use began to escalate, he enjoyed it and the people that smoked it:

> I also liked the camaraderie among pot smokers. We would all get together and smoke a joint and it would feel really good. It also was a great way for a shy teenager like me to talk to a girl. When I had pot, they seemed to like me, so I started dealing. It was really two-bit stuff, I never made any money off it and never learned how to grow it.

Sean confessed that what he got from pot smoking, mostly, was a reputation and little more: "Instead I just gained a reputation, because of that the bullies wouldn't mess with me and the girls seemed to like me."

By the time he was sixteen, Sean felt like he needed to have marijuana or alcohol to get to sleep. Although he struggled in school, he was bright enough to continue passing and knew he was going on to college.

In high school, Sean had many jobs, including working at a local restaurant and fast food place, and performing janitorial and maintenance work. When he went to college, Sean wanted to get as far away as possible from his family, whom he did not get along with:

> My parents had marital problems. I think sometimes I was a scapegoat for those problems [...] I had to get away. I got some money and I was really excited about getting away to college, but things got out of hand very fast.

According to Sean, his drinking and pot smoking escalated when he reached college, to the point where he was failing out. He could not maintain steady work. At the time, Sean was seventeen years old. As with Bernard, Sean's use of drugs was escalated by his proximity to a party lifestyle.

> Salvation City is one heck of a chance to grow up in. Yeah [...] everything was available. And when you factor in the time and the place, there was nobody to say no and nobody to place limits on how much I did, except the police. Since I was never looking for any trouble with anybody, never got into any fights, flew below radar, I never got into any trouble with the police.

At eighteen years old, Sean attended a party where there was unlimited alcohol. He arrived at the party with a friend, but when the friend started to speak to other people, Sean was left alone.

> I started drinking that night. And the next afternoon I woke up on the floor of a stranger's house. I was wearing sunglasses and Sony Walkman headphones. I don't know how I got there [...] then someone explained to me that I got so drunk that I was yelling at a girl who had a bottle of wine and I was asking her to pour her wine into my cup. She wouldn't because I had beer in there already.

According to Sean, some people dragged him out that night and took him to a friend of a friend's house so that he would not be arrested. Sean went to college in a dry county (one where alcohol is not allowed) outside of Salvation City. It was partially his choice. He wanted to get away from his parents' house and avoid all the temptations of drug use that were present in Salvation City. On his first day, while checking into the campus housing, Sean met a college student and was invited to a party where there was open drug use and alcohol. He confessed to being high several days or weeks after his first college partying experience. Although Sean struggled in college for two years, he maintained minimally passing grades. Whenever he fell into legal trouble, such as bouncing numerous checks around town, he scrambled and took various odd jobs to pay off his bills and avoid prosecution.

> Because my bills were paid and I was at least passing in college, I thought I was really doing good. I'd tell people that I was working going to college. I paid my bills and I was not dependent on anybody for rent or my living expenses. Of course, I wound up living in rat holes. But I figured that's what young guys do and didn't complain much.

When Sean was twenty-two and in his fourth year of college, he was struggling so much in school that he transferred to a college in Salvation City and returned home. One of the first things that Sean remembered about his move back home was that one of his major sources of drugs had been arrested and was in jail. He felt that it would be safe for to him to return to Salvation City because with his former drug dealer in jail, he could not be subpoenaed. Still, Sean had no intention of quitting drugs.

When Sean was twenty-two, a very close friend almost died in a drug-related incident. This is one of the things that he attributed his sobriety to today:

> [...] a friend of mine was taking LSD. She nearly fell to her death. She was hanging over a railing at her apartment complex, three stories up. I went to the hospital, worried about her, and proceeded to lecture her about her unhealthy lifestyle and the drugs would kill her. I knew that she had a serious problem.

Sean said that she, along with a boyfriend, retorted with the statement, "Sean, we don't have a problem with drugs, *you* do."

By his early twenties, Sean had already been to the doctor several times with various gastric problems and abdominal pains brought on by unknown causes. "I told the doctor that I was just going to college and working and that led to a lot of stress. The doctor did not believe me and said that I was clearly doing unhealthy things to my body."

Shortly after that, Sean borrowed his parents' car and accidentally left marijuana in it. His father found the drugs and spoke to his mother. Sean's parents were so concerned about his problems that they told him that they thought they would save his life by calling the police. At the time, Sean had a sheet with a hundred hits of LSD in his house, but his parents did not discover it or call the police. Still, he was told he was doing irreparable damage to his body. It was obvious to him: "They didn't know how to get me to stop drugs. I was dying, I was vomiting, I had blood in my stool."

At age twenty-four, Sean promised his mother that he would get help. He went to a Narcotics Anonymous (NA) meeting, thinking that he would get some tips on how to cut down on his drug use. He figured it would get him to stay out of trouble: "And I really did want to cut down. I decided to quit cold turkey for a couple of weeks, and I even attended a few more meetings, but eventually went back to drinking."

Sean admitted that he felt embarrassed that he went back to drinking, so he decided to go back to NA. One of Sean's early experiences with NA involved him being invited to stay in a halfway house, although he was not aware of it at the time. "I remember a guy that made an impression on me at one of the NA meetings." According to Sean, the NA member told him that he had to move out of his apartment because living alone for him was not a good thing. The NA member told him that he needed to live in a nice place and he recommended that Sean move in with a few people that were trying to get their act together:

> I thought what the heck, it would be cheaper than when I was living alone. It only took me a couple of days to come to my senses.

Sean gradually realized that he had committed himself to six months in a Salvation City halfway house. Life at the house at first proved to be difficult for Sean:

> There was one guy who I was really jealous of. Because he was living off of a disability check due to his mental illness. He would watch TV all the time, groan and make weird noises, and sleep whenever he wanted to and stay up whenever he wanted to. I was jealous of him, really, I guess, because I needed a rest myself. I was working and also trying to finish up college. I mean, I was going to be a college graduate and I didn't want to be living with this loser.

Sean went on to tell about his displeasure with the first few weeks in a halfway house:

> There was this other guy and he thought he was the big shot because he had about two months more clean time than me. He would talk about how we should pool our money together and save money on groceries, but I would still be nice to him because he drove pizza delivery and gave me a discount on pizza. But I really didn't like him and I was mad at him all the time.

Sean also said that there was one person that he really admired at the halfway house:

> He had almost a year clean and sober and he actually used to own a home and he was married once and I thought he had all this wisdom. About four months into my stay at the halfway house, I'd saved 300 bucks and that son of a bitch stole it from me. He was a no good con artist.

Sean went on to say that his NA sponsor at the time told him that there was nothing he could do about it. His sponsor said that if he tried to hurt the thief, it would only result in either expulsion from the halfway house or legal difficulties.

Sean never did learn to like the halfway house, but attributed his current sobriety to the highly regulated conditions:

> My friends that drank wouldn't come in the house and I hated the house, but guess what? I got almost one year sober. Maybe this crap I went through was exactly what I needed to get on my feet. I hated the meetings, I hated having to answer or worry about what might happen in the house. But I stayed clean also.

Today, Sean has twenty-three years clean and sober. People who do not know him very well would never think that he had ever had any type of problem. Instead, most people think of him as squeaky clean. He is a role model in Salvation City for many. He sponsors a local Little League baseball team and is head coaches of his child's team as well

Sean is active in Salvation City's halfway house programs, visiting them and participating in outreach. Frequently, the residents of the halfway houses look at him and wonder why he does that, thinking that he has nothing in common with them. Yet, he is quick to point out, whether they believe him or not, that he has been in a place quite similar to them.

Sean's final statement was: "If they hang in there, they'll have a better life."

CONCLUSION: SALVATION CITY'S ETHICAL DILEMMA

An ethnography of Salvation City's halfway house residents gives us insight into the sociology of halfway houses. We have discussed halfway house issues with many other residents in several phases of treatment and aftercare, many of whose stories bore similarities to the ones above. We have also talked to several residents who have been admitted or committed to different types of halfway houses, mainly work release and drug treatment. Although we do not have enough data to make bold generalizations, we feel that it is important to stress the commonalities among the successful cases, as well as the commonalities among the failures.

Here, we list the commonalities among successes. We observe that halfway house success stories follow a pattern which centers primarily on the resident's own desire to reform, coupled with an appropriately staffed program. The following are some of the commonalities among success stories:

1. In halfway house successes, houses provided opportunities for individuals who wanted to take advantage of their circumstances and rehabilitate. For example, in Sean's case, the halfway house allowed him to live cheaply and return to college.
2. It is not important whether a person is committed to treatment through a formal system or self-admitted. For example, Jane, who was admitted to a halfway house, turned out to be a success story. Bernard, who committed himself voluntarily, continues to suffer.

3. In each success story, halfway house clients complained of suffering hardships, such as having to adhere to the institutional regulations and of staff members or other residents who would place them in monitoring. From this, one observes that rehabilitation is not about immediate comfort and "customer satisfaction." It is about providing services that can assist perceived societal outcasts in their attempt to return to society.

4. Each success story also documented a strict regimen, or some social controls in place, that success cases adhered to. The residents were told what to do and had to follow a specific program. In some cases, like Sean's, the other residents seemed to regulate one another's behavior more than the institution did.

5. In success cases, houses were staffed with supportive personnel. There is a need for this in the recovery process due to its complex nature. Recovery is a long-term procedure. Several participants in our interviews reported that there was at least one staff member that they severely disliked. However, they came to realize that the actions of that individual were necessary for their recovery. In contrast, Bernard's case provided an example of staff members who may have been overly accommodating in allowing him to return to work when he was not ready.

People like Bernard, regardless of any treatment they go through, might always have problems with drug addiction and alcoholism. It is clear that Bernard, the only failure that we have reported on, placed his obligation to his career above recovery. It is obvious that people accept their lifestyles if they are willing to deal with stress in their own particular way.

On the other hand, there are success stories like Jane and Sean, who really wanted to quit abusing drugs and alcohol and who placed rehabilitation above all else. It is also apparent that there is no correlation between voluntary entrance to a halfway house and continued sobriety. In Jane's case, she was committed from a psychiatric hospital to a halfway house as part of an aftercare program. Bernard and Sean, on the other hand, admitted themselves to halfway houses. Despite the fact that they both entered programs of their own volition, their choice did not result in the same outcome. None of the interviewees reported that they enjoyed their stay. None reported that they formed lifelong friendships with other residents. However, the safety of the atmosphere and the supervised daily activities offered each of these individuals an opportunity to get clean and sober. It is clear that long-term sobriety is a long-term project. None of the individuals were "cured" through the programs. They were merely given the opportunities to live in a safe environment and avoid many of the behaviors that got them in trouble. They spent less time with bad influences. In addition, at these houses they were visited by supportive people from the outside who served as their support systems for long-term recovery. Finally, several addicts and alcoholics in recovery recounted stories that expressed that they did not like a lot of things about halfway houses. Among the common themes was resentment of rules and being told what to do. However, the majority acknowledged that although they were not doing what they wanted, the structure contributed to their recovery.

As one program staffer stated:

> They complain about every single thing under the sun. It's a simple program and when I work, I break it down, really simple. Number one: you don't bring drugs into the house. You know, there is just a core group of rules I have, and it's no violence, threatening, drugs. I make them watch their language and curfew. You know, if you just go to work, do your job, do their meetings, then I don't have a problem. But I think they do get better. They get better on their own or it's like everything I've ever done. What you put into it is what you get out of it.
>
> (Personal interview: Sean)

CHAPTER 4

WHY WE DON'T NEED
HALFWAY HOUSES

There are emotional and logical objections to the idea that halfway houses are necessary social institutions. The first objection is emotionally driven and heartfelt. It cites the victims of former addicts and convicts who failed to rehabilitate in halfway houses and went on to cause harm to the communities around them. It involves homeowners, shopowners, and other residents of neighborhoods where halfway houses are sited against popular demand.

Nearly two-thirds of all convicts recidivate within three years of their release from prison. Because it is uncertain as to whether or not addicts will actually rehabilitate in halfway houses, it is reasonable to assume that transitional residences have the potential to act as hot spots for criminal activity or drug use. Hubbard et al. (2001) reported that two-thirds of those treated for heroin addiction resume use within one month of detoxification. Many argue that placing ex-convicts or addicts into communities is like putting a wolf among sheep. At some level, one at least owes an apology to the sheep.

Of course, some halfway houses do not house dangerous residents. These our central argument does not address; however, we point out that the majority of halfway houses are run by state-funded correctional agencies that deal with known criminal populations. Even for halfway houses that specialize in non-criminal residents, there remain numerous problems with service delivery and community safety.]

THE EMOTIONAL ARGUMENT

From June 2006 to November of 2006, Stephen Hayes and Joshua Komisarjevsky spent considerable amounts of time together at both Berman House Treatment Center (a Connecticut Department of Correction residential facility mainly focused on substance abusers) and Silliman House (a 24-bed work-release program) in Hartford, Connecticut. Both Berman House and Silliman House are halfway houses where ex-convicts receive a variety of social services, but each has a specified function. Berman House specializes in substance abuse problems and is often the first Connecticut halfway house that residents are placed in before entering work release programs such as Silliman House.

Both Hayes and Komisarjevsky were subject to random tests for drugs and alcohol. According to house administrators Community Solutions Incorporated, both were in line with program policy until Hayes tested positive for drugs in November of 2006 and was sent back to prison until May of 2007. Komisarjevsky, on the other hand, successfully completed his stint at the halfway house and returned to his mother's home.

While incarcerated at Silliman House, Hayes and Komisarjevsky spent quality time with each other. According to other residents, the men planned to enter work together as independent home contractors upon release from the facility and were trying to obtain contracts to work on houses almost immediately after Hayes was released from prison.

Both men seemed like ideal halfway house candidates. Both were non-violent offenders with drug addiction issues. Hayes, age forty-four, was the father of two teenagers. Komisarjevsky, age twenty-six, was from a privileged family and engaged in a custody battle for his daughter.

Both were employed, lived with their mothers, and generally followed the terms of their parole. Both also lived with their families in what was considered a relatively stable environment.

Although they spent no prison time together, apparently their meeting at the halfway house was enough to begin their working relationship. Their initial business venture regarded not home repair, but home invasion. This venture began within three days of the removal of Komisarjevsky's electronic monitoring device by the Connecticut Department of Probation.

The two men were "strange bedfellows," as defined by a Silliman housemate, "John," who asked to remain anonymous:

> *The old and fat one was kind of an extrovert. He used to spend a bunch of time talking about whores and the different things he do to em. Always a big mouth* [...] blabbing about his bullshit [...] *you couldn't tell whether he was going to go off the edge or play it straight. He probably could've conned his PO for a while if he wouldn't have got popped on the piss test. Most of us do anyway. You* know, it's *the iron law* [...].
>
> (Personal interview with John, an ex-convict)

Hayes made a point to tell other inmates in the halfway house that he could not believe how "lucky" he was to be released on parole. With over twenty prison disciplinary violations and a record extending back to 1980, Hayes had a hard time fathoming why the parole board in Connecticut let him see a glimpse of freedom before the end of his sentence.

Perhaps it was also lucky for Komisarjevsky that, unlike Hayes, he successfully completed his halfway house residency. John said that Komisarjevsky was simply "not right in the head," he was surprised that an odd (yet charismatic) character like Komiskarjevsky survived in prison. The prison law about keeping out of other convicts' business also applies in the halfway house, so comments gleaned from John were sparse. He did, however, indicate disrespect for the other man:

> The other one [Komisarjevsky] was a punk [...] would've been turned out [raped] in a second at Northern [State Penitentiary].

I know a bunch of motherfuckers who hope they let them loose in the population there right now [laughs]. He liked to think of himself as a predator, but everybody knew he was just a little weird. He wasn't hard. He was always whining about how women fucked up his life.

THE PETIT INCIDENT

Cheshire, Connecticut is a traditional upper-middle class township with a population of approximately 30,000 people. During the summer, Cheshire is an idyllic place, where high-priced colonial homes are framed by well-manicured lawns. Its residents have felt safety from violent criminal activities for many years. An accurate account of the Cheshire home invasion and its aftermath is a microcosm of the emotional fervor on both sides in the battle over the necessity of halfway houses.

At approximately 3 a.m. on July 26, 2007, two men (who were introduced to each other by the Connecticut Department of Correction) emerged from a pickup truck wearing hooded masks and two layers of gloves to conceal any fingerprints they might leave behind. Earlier in the week, they had spotted a well-dressed middle-aged woman with her 17-year-old daughter in tow at a local grocery store. After tailing the couple home to their Cheshire residence, the two men decided to burglarize the old colonial home.

Perhaps the two men considered that Dr. William Petit his wife, Janet Hawke-Petit, or their two children, Hayley (age 17) and Michaela (age 11), would wake up during the attempted burglary. Perhaps they counted on it. Hayes carried a modified air rifle purchased at Wal-Mart in case he ran into any heavy resistance from the doctor. Komisarjevsky allegedly carried an aluminum baseball bat and heavy electrical wires to subdue and restrain if necessary.

The men proceeded to enter the Petit house through a basement window, bludgeoning the doctor with the bat. After subduing the doctor, the two men covered his body with a garbage bag, tied him with the electrical wires, and left him in the basement, perhaps assuming that he was dying. The two men then tied Hawke-Petit and her daughters to their beds, severed the house phone lines, and proceeded to sexually assault the mother and her two daughters while the doctor lay unconscious and bleeding.

> Komisarjevsky had a lot of trouble with sexual relationships in the past. In 2002, he had gotten his 15-year-old girlfriend pregnant. He was entrenched in a custody battle. Much to his annoyance, his new 18-year-old girlfriend had also relocated to Arkansas without his consent. Komisarjevsky vented his anger on the Petit girls, allegedly raping Michaela and forcing her to stand in the shower while he took pictures with a cell phone.

In the early morning, the pair tied the Petit children to their beds once again. Hayes commandeered the Petits' vehicle and appropriated several canisters of gasoline that would later be used to torch the home, stopping off at his own truck to stash several items stolen during the invasion. Afterward, the two men made Janet Hawke-Petit phone her husband's office and inform them that the doctor would not be at work that day. They then ordered her to drive them to a local bank and withdraw $10,000. Hawke-Petit made a withdrawal for $15,000, perhaps hoping the extra $5,000 would spare lives or that the bank teller would notice the covert message that she left on the withdrawal slip. The teller did, and notified her superior, who then called the Cheshire police.

About a half hour later, back at the Petit residence, a house burglary evolved into the murder of almost an entire family. Komisarjevsky, in his taped statement to investigators, claimed that Hayes began to get violent with Mrs. Hawke-Petit. The two invaders wanted no witnesses left behind. They splashed the gasoline and lit a fire on their way out of the home.

By this time, the area had come to life with police activity due to the incident at the bank. But it was too late. According to police sources, the two men appeared in a frenzied mood as they pulled out of the Petit driveway in Mrs. Petit's vehicle with Komisarjevsky at the wheel. It was not long before they noticed the presence of the police roadblock at the end of the street. In a scene that might have been straight out of a Hollywood screenplay, Komisarjevsky attempted to smash through a blockade of Cheshire police cruisers. He learned shortly after that this only works in movies. The adrenaline pumped for the officers as they surrounded the two gloved and hooded men emerging from the crippled vehicle.

Petit had made it through the invasion with his life, but badly beaten. At some time during or before the fire he was able to escape from his basement through the outer hatch (the fire escape hatch in his basement), but not soon enough to save the lives of his three loved ones. He was taken to a hospital with severe head wounds shortly afterwards.

The Aftermath

After what Connecticut residents have come to know as simply "the Petit Invasion," state legislators reacted quickly. Crime control advocates rallied and within a month Connecticut governor M. Jodi Rell placed a moratorium on parole for all offenders in the state that was to last until November of 2008. Officials at the Connecticut Office of Policy Management (OPM) and the Connecticut Department of Correction began a full-scale attempt to reevaluate the state's probation and parole process. The Connecticut Department of Corrections is, as of this writing, also pursuing a full-scale investigation into its halfway house system.

But is this Enough?

Dr. William Petit, at one time a revered endocrinologist, has not practiced medicine as of this writing. The children will never regain their lives, nor will Petit regain the family and home that he worked all his life to build. The Petit family, along with the entire Cheshire community, will never be the same. There is a strong emotional mark left by such incidents that results in people and communities feeling a sense of alienation and general distrust in the criminal justice system.

Said George, age twenty-six, a graduate student and local Cheshire resident:

> I knew the mother. She did a lot of great things for the community and everyone who knew her simply loved her. They should let

those guys out into the general population [prison population] and give them the poor man's death penalty.

(Personal interview: George)

George's voice, along with countless others, exuded emotion. He suggested that more people should be able to defend themselves by maintaining within their households (and sometimes concealing) firearms, but he was at a loss for words when asked about what the criminal justice system can do to make communities safer.

Many people, including those in the media, pointed to the backgrounds of Hayes and Komisarjevsky in trying to ascertain the cause of such aberrant behavior. However, except for a brief mention of it in two articles that appeared shortly after the incident, those people often failed to observe that shared time at a halfway house might have been an integral factor in the events that occurred. That being said, perhaps it is true that the childhood stories of both offenders are far more interesting than their institutional arrangements.

It is well known that our criminal justice system has become dysfunctional in many ways. That is, it has become an institution leading to more of the problem that it is supposed to solve (in this case, crime). Halfway houses, like other correctional institutions, afford opportunities for deliberation between criminal minds during a unique phase of the criminal's correctional supervision. The cultural importation hypothesis is among the oldest idea in penology (Bentham 1763) and suggests that where criminals aggregate, they will bring shared discussion of crime. It has not seemed more than coincidental to many people that when ex-convicts come together, their mindset on criminal activity, with one foot in the free world and one foot in the correctional world, that they will begin to think thoughts of their old lives and whatever emotional gratitude was received therein.

Many argue that the official reaction to the Petit Invasion was primarily "lip service" and followed by no effective action. This is probably not the case. By the spring of 2008, the state's jail and prison system was full to 175 percent capacity because of parole revocations. Although the loss of the Petit family was a tragedy that can never be truly corrected, the state's reaction was both swift and severe.

The argument we offer here is an emotional one. Simply stated: if at all responsible, even in the least way, for events that occurred that summer night, halfway houses should not be allowed to exist. Some might argue that when Komisarjevsky and Hayes planned to go into business together as home contractors, there was a shared understanding that such an arrangement would provide a wonderful front for a casing operation. More or less detailed statements from ex-convicts who spent time around them confirm this.

An important point to be emphasized is that such events can have tragic effects on the psychology of people in one's community. The seeming randomness of the occurrence of such an event is frightening. Residents of Cheshire now lead a different lifestyle, locking their doors at night and spending vast sums of money on home security systems.

Some argue that if prisons are like elementary schools, then halfway houses are finishing schools. Like schools, halfway houses afford inmates a place to congregate in a relatively informed and free environment. For Hayes and Komisarjevsky, the halfway house was also a business school and a networking opportunity. Hayes was the muscle and Komisarjevsky the brains of the operation. One man, a potential customer of Hayes and Komisarjevsky, noted that Komisarjevsky did all the talking. The customer came to the conclusion that Hayes and Komisarjevsky were potential con men and did not enlist their services.

Some argue that there is no room in communities for these finishing schools. Had the two men been on straight parole, they would have never met. We argue that in this case Dr. William Petit's life would not have been destroyed and his three loved ones' lives not taken. To add to the emotionally charged argument over halfway houses is the idea of justice for both the victims and the community. In May of 2008, the Petit home was demolished and enshrined (Wittenburg, 2008). It stands as a reminder to the community of an unholy alliance founded by two criminals in a Hartford halfway house.

Of the Petit family, a 2007 *Hartford Courant* article had the following to report:

> Hayley, who raised $54,000 for the Multiple Sclerosis Society in honor of her mother, longed to be a doctor like her dad. She would have turned 18 on Oct. 15. She had been accepted at Dartmouth, her father's alma mater. Michaela, who was following in her sister's footsteps as an MS fundraiser, loved to cook. She would have turned 12 on Nov. 17. (Poitras, Altimari, & Tuohy, 2007) The article continues:

> The two girls now flank their mother in small graves facing the woods in the rear of Plainville's West Cemetery. Personal tokens that friends have placed on the raw earth serve as solemn tributes to the Petit women.

This was a tragic waste of life. The crime resulted from a chance meeting of criminal minds in the Connecticut halfway house system. The halfway house gave these criminals a chance to share their ideas about starting a home repair business as a front for criminal operations that would involve breaking and entering. Had the two criminals escaped, they would have undoubtedly committed more crimes and perhaps taken more lives.

THE EMPIRICAL ARGUMENTS

The second line of argument against halfway houses as necessary social institutions is not so emotional. It involves empirical facts about halfway houses. Their cost, their presence in economically struggling areas, their symbolism, and, last but not least, their residents' characteristics have all been taken into account in previous scientific literature. From this scientific literature, we can ascertain several good reasons why halfway houses are undesirable for communities as a collective.

Community residents often claim that they are victimized by the siting of halfway houses and that they want to keep these homes out of their areas (Piat, 2000a). Among their primary concerns are personal security (Rabkin et al., 1984), declining property values (Dear, 1977; Farber,

1986; Myers & Bridges, 1995; Scott & Scott, 1980), and a general negative impact on neighborhood amenities and quality of life in the community (Eynon, 1989; Baron & Piasecki, 1981).

The most common emphasis in scientific literature involving halfway houses has been on successful and unsuccessful completion. The literature has historically been focused on individual characteristics and how they relate to success rate, both during the halfway house stay and after. However, much of this research does not look at the halfway house itself as a theoretical predictor of future criminality.

Of those words that look at halfway houses as predictors of recidivism or desistance (the withdrawal from criminal activity), there are mixed results. Some findings specify that there are certain social and demographic factors indicating that individual predispositions toward drug and alcohol abuse, along with parole to a halfway house, are indicators of recidivism. Other works have actually shown a positive relationship between recidivism and halfway houses. There are methodological issues to these studies, of course.

Because these studies are primarily concerned with whether halfway houses work or not in reducing recidivism, they fail to recognize the bigger picture. That is the picture of the community that is burdened with the halfway house. Halfway houses are filled with residents who are more likely to recidivate than not. Below, several reasons are offered that suggest that the practice of transitional residence in halfway houses must be abandoned. Among them are the financial burdens of halfway houses that the taxpayer must bear the brunt of.

1. HALFWAY HOUSES PRESENT FINANCIAL BURDENS

The first and most simple argument we offer against the halfway house involves the financial burdens of halfway houses on state and local taxpayers. Halfway houses are almost as costly as prisons to the taxpayer. As such, the fact should be taken into consideration that they are statistically no more effective than straight parole (which is generally a less expensive alternative) in reducing recidivism rates.

A 1975 technical report, commissioned by the Correctional Economic Center in affiliation with the now defunct Law Enforcement Assistance Administration, indicated that there are four types of costs associated with the implementation of halfway houses. These are criminal justice system costs, costs external to the criminal justice system, opportunity costs incurred by halfway house residents, and costs to the community in which the halfway house is located.

Criminal justice system costs, in most cases, refer to real estate costs and utilities as well as payment for personnel, which may include directors, assistant directors, community resource managers, counselors, secretaries, bookkeepers, cooks and housekeepers, professional fees and contract services, and maintenance personnel. Additionally, there are costs for items such as toiletries and food.

There are three types of external costs that can be incurred by halfway houses. These are: educational or vocational services provided by external agencies, drug treatment/detoxification services provided by external agencies, and mental health services. The earliest research into halfway houses proved that the majority of external costs are medical in nature. Detoxification services, drug treatment, and the hiring of clinical personnel external to the criminal justice system prove an immense burden to the taxpayer.

Opportunity costs and costs to the community are not as easy to measure and are the source of much theoretical speculation. Opportunity costs are best understood as costs that are associated with the client's leisure and work activities. Transportation for clients is essential, especially when they are in the early stages of job hunting.

In addition, there are three types of alleged costs to the community in which the halfway house is located: tax loss associated with property managed by nonprofit residences, decline in property values in the neighborhood in which a house is located, and the cost of new crimes committed by the clients of a house.

Although there has recently been no research effort to weigh the costs and benefits of 'halfway houses nationally, a recent study of Connecticut's Department of Correction contracted halfway house system indicated that the combined estimated annual budget for Connecticut's largest cities was in excess of $13 million. The study also reported that the entire cost only provided the state with a total of 1009 beds.

Among Connecticut's largest providers, the average cost per bed is approximately $12,000 per year, which is near the average cost of tuition at a Connecticut state school. Offenders on straight parole are directly held responsible for their residences, making straight parole a far cheaper option.

Although the Connecticut study may not be generalizable to all states, there are purely financial reasons to abandon halfway houses if one chooses to argue for that position. Such money could be used to fund underprivileged children to make sure that they are not sucked into a vacuum of criminality, as has been so common in underprivileged communities. Successful treatment programs are personnel intensive, highly structured, and very costly. Private residential drug and alcohol treatment program costs range from $55.00 per day per offender in Massachusetts to $61.00 in Colorado. Texas has invested in public treatment facilities which can cost as much as $80.00 per day per offender. In comparison, prison costs in California are about $60.00 per day and jail costs are about $55.00 per day.

In addition to paying state parole officers who must monitor the clientele of halfway houses, money must also be shared between house owners, house service providers, and other essential personnel. In over thirty studies of halfway houses, we encountered mixed results regarding the halfway house as a sound fiscal alternative to either incarceration or parole. We note in this context that deep economic strains currently confronting state and local governments throughout the U.S. raise challenges that will force decision makers to make critical funding decisions. At some level, the funding of halfway houses becomes a question of financial sustainability.

Although the cost of maintaining an inmate in prison ($32,000 annually) exceeds the cost of placing an inmate in a halfway house, such money might be otherwise used to build and maintain one minimum-security facility that could house a total of 1009 inmates. So, with regard to this point, it is important to ask the questions: "Why the middleman? Why the extra step?"

The strongest argument is, of course, because the halfway house is not a proven remedy to recidivism. To this end, a review of the relevant literature was conducted and revealed mixed findings. Metraux and Culhane (2004) found that 32.8 percent of a New York reentry cohort who participated in halfway houses were rearrested within two years of release. Other findings by Kelly and Welsh (2008) indicated that individual predispositions toward drug and alcohol abuse, *along with parole to a halfway house*, were strong and positive indicators of recidivism. Still other research by Bonta et al. (2008) suggested that halfway houses with lower success rates had a lack of staff integrity and also were plagued by probation/parole officers who spent too much time on the enforcement aspect of supervision and not enough time on the service delivery role of supervision.

There is also the idea of social justice, which might suggest that halfway houses are humane alternatives to either straight parole or incarceration. Although this is not a fiscally based argument, there is the suggestion that somehow the halfway house transcends mere economics. We admit to a degree that this is true. However, consider the following: halfway houses provide services for ex-convicts that might otherwise be directed to crime prevention programs, or other social programs that provide better services for impoverished communities. In this light, it would seem that halfway houses are not a good long- or short-term investment.

2. HALFWAY HOUSES LOWER PROPERTY VALUE AND PERCEIVED COMMUNITY VALUE

A second argument that is empirically based and refutes the practice of funding transitional residences for former prisoners revolves around both economics and perceived safety. A major type of literature in halfway house research regards geographic siting of halfway houses and the effects of such placement on neighborhood residents. A common theme in the literature on halfway houses is the NIMBY ("not in my backyard") phenomenon, which involves the community-based siting of transitional residences.

The debate about halfway house placement in communities is almost as controversial as the argument of whether transitional residences are effective in reducing recidivism. Some advocates of halfway houses argue that halfway house placement increases community safety. The argument central to this idea is that halfway houses improve the quality of life in a given area by attracting law enforcement and social service providers to that area.

The majority of arguments against halfway houses emphasize the fact that residential community correctional centers cluster many known career felons into one area, providing criminal networking opportunities and contributing to general neighborhood crime rates and decay. Although no study has yet been done of halfway houses and their effects on property value over time, a Columbia University study of North Carolina home prices indicated a correlation between lower property values and registered sex offenders in the vicinity. It is reasonable to assume that halfway houses affect community property values in the same way that registered sex offenders tend to.

There is also evidence that perceived safety and well-being of residents is reduced by the placement of halfway houses near their residence. NIMBY responses are often inspired by the placement of facilities such as drug treatment centers, mental health facilities, detention centers, affordable housing, and homeless shelters that serve small sectors of the population (Schively, 2007). Johnson (2006) focused on the perceptions of communities in Pittsburgh. He used a mathematical model that showed that placement in affluent communities would be beneficial for transitional residence participants, but he also acknowledged that such moves would be met with negative community perceptions.

Although there is no clear peer-reviewed evidence that halfway houses reduce property values in certain areas, there is much evidence that they contribute to a general loss of faith in the criminal justice system's legitimacy. Much previous literature has focused on the importance of perceived safety versus real safety by asking the question: "Is it more important for people to feel safe or actually be safe?"

A recent quote by Senator John Whitmire of Houston reads as follows: "Almost nobody wants a halfway house full of convicted felons in their neighborhood, so we almost never get a new one [...] The waiting lists get longer and longer." (Ward, 2004)

A November 5, 2007 *Hartford Courant* interview with a disgruntled resident recorded these feelings:

> There are hundreds more of these bastards in our communities. I live in New Haven, and I can't believe how many group homes are being injected into our neighborhoods. Hopefully someone will look at the revolving doors of the criminal justice system and mental health systems in our state.

Although many are ready to dismiss such a reaction as overzealous, it is important to note that most halfway houses are likely to be sited in areas where there is already a great deal of perceived fear among residents about being victims of crime. In this case, property values seem trite compared to the well-being of law-abiding citizens.

Kraft and Clary (1991) argued that NIMBY responses are characterized by both parochial and localized attitudes toward the problem, which exclude broader implications as well as distrust of project sponsors. Attempted placement of transitional housing within communities is usually met with resistance (Segal, Baumohl & Moyles, 1980; Innes, 1993; Piat, 2000a; Cowan, 2003). Piat (2000a) emphasizes many ways in which residents can respond to placement issues including, but not limited to: letters to editors; door-to-door campaigns; petitions to legislators; and organized protesting and picketing.

They concluded that there are highly emotional responses to siting conflicts. It is important to note at this level the differences between real security and perceived security and to acknowledge that they are equally important in a social justice framework. Much recent literature on homeland security policies has focused on the idea that people need to feel secure more than they need to actually be secure.

Although the Hayes and Komisarjevsky incident did not involve a neighborhood where a halfway house was placed, it is easy to see what kind of turmoil such incidents can cause among residents of any community. It is highly probable that such incidents are more likely to occur in areas where halfway houses are placed. Of course, the majority of these incidents would probably not be as dramatic as the Cheshire incident, which in many ways resembles events discussed in popular literature such as Truman Capote's *In Cold Blood*. Problems such as simple breaking and entering, car theft, and open-air drug markets might be more common occurrences in communities with transitional residences.

Nevertheless, perceived safety is important to Cheshire residents. According to one resident, after the invasion, Cheshire turned into a "gun buying, door locking kind of place." (Personal interview: George) In addition, halfway houses may lower resident involvement in neighborhoods and contribute to neighborhood decay.

At its core, the concept of the halfway house proposes a funded haven for ex-convicts within communities. As such, placing halfway houses within communities tends to foster distrust toward authorities and general withdrawal from neighborhood activity. Community residents may feel coerced by agents of social control to accept the halfway house as part of that community. This may mean failures for local businesses, among other things. Under conditions of extreme economic uncertainty, coercion may not be a particularly efficacious mechanism for building viable communities and neighborhoods.

3. GENERAL INSTABILITY WITH INTENSIVE SUPERVISION

Criminologist James Byrne (1990) referenced intensive supervision as a "failed panacea." According to Byrne, cases that are processed for intensive supervision often do not fit individual circumstances. At the heart of the matter of funding for halfway houses lies the issue of adequate staffing and how intensive supervision for ex-convicts should be managed. Such administrative concerns are shared by correctional agencies that generally designate a representative parole officer to state run transitional services.

The ideal halfway house provides an array of services to clientele, ranging from drug addiction programs, to economic planning, to mental health needs. Although some research has been concerned with issues regarding service delivery for those on intensive probation or parole, little attention has been paid to the financial realities present. Although there are many altruistic reasons involved for running halfway houses, organizations that maintain halfway houses may need to cut corners to a certain extent. Likewise, funding problems for probation and parole departments may inhibit adequate staffing.

One veteran employee of a halfway house was open about the nature of his work. Although he clearly believed in the importance of his job and was happy to talk to us about his experiences working as a counselor, he was candid about the positive and negative experiences of the programs he worked for.

> Some cheat the programs while others are serious. I see a lot of abuse in the state programs […] just people getting all sorts of unnecessary things. But there are some people well-deserving getting what they need.

When we asked him about important programs that were effective in transitioning an individual towards independence, he said:

> Let's go with basic needs: people want to get out of their treatment facility to come to a living facility so they can get $100 voucher for clothes and $40 personal hygiene items and $50 for food while they're doing it, so that's 190 dollars just to leave treatment. So they come and say, can I get basic needs. So it's not just that one. And a lot of people are receiving benefits but are working under the table or maybe not paying their child support. Things that need to be reconciled. A lot of legal issues come in there. A lot, a lot of legal issues. We get some dual-diagnosed people that we are really not qualified to handle. We have people with problems, I mean a lot, a lot of problems. One time we had a gentleman that was overweight. And we said just substance abuse: we don't want to hear about overeating or gambling. If it's not substance abuse,

> it doesn't go in our treatment plans and it doesn't fit in our scope
> of treatment.
>
> (Personal interview: halfway house employee)

As stated above, one argument against halfway houses is rooted in the idea that halfway houses are an unnecessary middleman in the reentry process. With each transaction, taxpayer money moves away from the state capital and there is potential for the misuse or even abuse of state funding. One of the biggest ways to misuse funds allocated for halfway houses is to employ non-credentialed staff for services that are best handled professionally. For example, as one Department of Corrections official, who chose to remain anonymous, noted:

> There is a great deal of variance in halfway houses as we look
> across the state of Connecticut. Some of them are pretty good
> [...] but there are others who simply don't know what they're
> doing. It's funny how some of these houses have tried to pass off
> non-credentialed people as legitimate staff. In terms of providing
> services, it would seem infinitely more sensible to maintain con-
> trol of these funds at the state level.

Staff integrity is a question in many halfway houses. A recent Supreme Court case illustrates how transitional residences without substantial staff integrity can lead to problems. With reference to the case of *Correctional Services Corp. v. Malesko* (2001), we point out an incident of a halfway house resident with a heart condition who was forced by a correctional officer to climb five flights of stairs and suffered a heart attack.

A major type of literature involves a general assessment of institutional characteristics associated with community corrections and how these characteristics are related to dual completion. An early entry in this field was put forth by Gumrukcu (1968), who suggested that staff-patient interaction quality was a strong predictor of success in mental health-specific halfway houses. Piquero (2003), in an analysis of Maryland's community probation program, indicated that "social bonding" was likely to curb recidivism among offenders reentering the community.

Many researchers have advanced the idea that the functional environment of a halfway house is more important than the characteristics of the offenders who inhabit it. Along similar lines, Lowenkamp et al. (2006) used the Correctional Program Assessment Inventory (CPAI) (also see Gendreau & Andrews, 1996) to facilitate an evaluation of thirty-eight Ohio halfway houses. The researchers found that failures in program implementation, such as cost-effectiveness of the program, were important as significant predictors of offenders' readmission to prisons for new crimes.

In addition, as is the case with prisons, many discontented residents find solidarity in their mutual contempt for the halfway house setting. This contempt may augment the prisoners' bonding experience. Still, there is the possibility that staff may be inadequate. While people are placed on intensive supervision, there is generally an understanding that adequate personnel should heavily monitor clients. With regard to the Hayes and Komisarjevsky case, one can argue that if appropriate halfway house staff had been hired at the halfway houses they resided at, the true crisis could have been averted. It is perhaps true that a clinically trained psychologist or clinical sociologist could have detected problems with the risk of returning the two criminals to society. However, practicing clinicians are expensive and not a luxury that most halfway houses can afford.

Financial problems notwithstanding, there are also problems with intensive supervision that makes spotting risks a difficult job. This is a problem that even the most experienced clinicians may not detect. Again, we point out that Komisarjevsky and Hayes were ideal candidates for both halfway house residency and intensive supervision. Komisarjevsky was working at a roofing company that had just given him a promotion before the end of his electronic monitoring. Hayes also held down a job. Furthermore, Komisarjevsky had only served one period of incarceration and his record involved only a minimal level of aggression. To add to his credibility, Komisarjevsky was also awarded custody of his daughter about a month before the Petit home invasion. Hayes was also considered a minimum-security offender with a minimal violence history.

To underscore the margin of error regarding intensive supervision, it can be pointed out that parole officers with tremendous caseloads oversee the majority of intensive supervisions. There are 4.2 million people on probation in the United States and another three quarters of a million on parole. This makes it hard for even the most experienced parole officer to deliver quality service.

We argue that most halfway houses and transitional residences are venues for poor, low-quality service provisions. There are exceptions, such as rehabilitation centers for the wealthy. However, in general, we feel that the halfway house setting facilitates low-quality service due to its fiscal and administrative limitations. Agencies find it necessary to cut corners when they can due to their small budgets.

4. HALFWAY HOUSES BRING AGGREGATES OF CRIMINALS TOGETHER AND INCREASE OPPORTUNITIES FOR CRIMINAL NETWORKING

One of the enduring criticisms of correctional institutions revolves around the ideas of learning and labeling. The earliest penal reformers, such as Jeremy Bentham, referred to a process of "contamination" (Bentham, 2009 [1830]) among inmates. As described in Chapter Two, contamination refers to how prisoners share ideas that are criminal in nature. The first correctional institutions were built according to the principle of keeping prisoners isolated and separate. Darrell Steffensmeier's book *The Fence* (1986) chronicles how a young boy placed in a juvenile institution (and later a prison) learns the arts of both burglary and fencing (buying and reselling of stolen property). The idea of the prison as a learning institution applies to the halfway house as well. So does the idea of labeling, a theoretical concept which involves a person's accepting an identity as a secondary deviant, thus becoming more criminal in each contact with the system.

The idea of learning through contact with others is prevalent in our concern with halfway house residency. Although ex-offenders on regular parole probably do not have to struggle to find themselves in a position that enables criminal networking, they are also monitored to ensure that they stay away from places that contain heavy criminal aggregations. For criminal halfway house residents, the opposite is true. Ironically, the halfway house in some ways is the antithesis of straight parole because it brings together entire populations of criminals. The same is true with the substance-abuse halfway house, which brings together aggregates of addicts.

Differential association, along with a host of other learning-based criminological theories, suggests that exposure to people who share criminal beliefs will result in further criminal behavior. Referencing the Cheshire incident proves to be a useful tool in this regard. Reports indicated that although Joshua Komiskarjevsky, a perpitrator in the Cheshire Home Invasion, did experience periodic depression as a child, he became drawn to the technical aspects of breaking and entering as a convict. In prison, he learned about night-vision goggles and how to use latex gloves to avoid fingerprints. Similarly, Hayes, before his initial incarceration, was reported to be "an extremely nervous kid" during the 1980s. One source reported that:

> Hayes was a drug thief. He had some pretty good opportunities to move upward in the world, but after his numerous prison stays, he changed. He was more interested with getting high than legitimate work. I think what happened in his life is common among a lot of short-term inmates. These guys go into the joint knowing that they can be out soon. They use a place to make connections [...].
>
> (Personal interview: former inmate)

The Cheshire situation is tantamount to a "graduation" for two former students from the class of 2007. There is every indication that Komisarjevsky viewed his stay in prison as a learning experience. Hayes, on the other hand, seemed to be more drawn toward a general retreat from life after prison. Both inmates took their learning experiences to another level when they planned the ultimate scheme to start their home repair company as a cover operation for burglary.

As an ancillary matter, we argue that the halfway house provides an environment where people who have accepted the "secondary deviant" label on the way out of incarceration can share the material that is learned in prison. As it is adopted here, the term secondary deviant refers to a person who has accepted the label that formal agencies of social control have given him or her. A common research theme in labeling is the idea that a person who has been socially labeled as a criminal will act in accord with social expectations. Some halfway house residents are already painfully aware of that deviant status and merely try to comply with orders from probation and parole.

In consideration of the argument against the state-run halfway house for criminal offenders, it is important to consider the grouping of secondary deviants who have presumably learned a great deal about committing crime from short prison stays. Some findings indicate that it is likely that ex-convicts will recidivate more often after short prison stays (von Hirsch, Bottoms, E Burney & Wikstrom, 1999). The acceptance of the secondary deviant label often leads to further criminal activity, which a stay in a halfway house may only exacerbate due to prolonged residential contact with the criminal justice system.

Generally, we feel that the halfway house has potential to act as a networking mechanism for learned criminals. In addition, because residents of halfway houses are often required to temporarily leave incarceration for work purposes, residents of halfway houses have ample opportunity to scout out suitable targets in the communities that surround them. The halfway house is an environment where the prison experience can become realized as a part of a person's past and new ventures can be planned for those that have accepted their lot in life as a career criminal.

SUMMARY: HALFWAY HOUSES ARE HALFWAY SOLUTIONS

A large body of research has shown that convicted felons are unlikely to be rehabilitated. Similar research has shown that addicts will relapse and that, despite advances in medical technology, dealing with mental health issues may not be useful. Two related questions emerge with regard to the issue of halfway houses: "Is money that could be better utilized being thrown away?" and "Why not cut out the middle man or the extra step?"

We acknowledge that, in theory, the halfway house provides a sound alternative to an extended incarceration or to straight parole. However, in practice, it is notable that most correctional halfway houses are not financially or administratively equipped to meet an ideal standard. Accordingly, we do not argue that the idea of the halfway house is a fundamentally bad one, but we do argue that halfway houses are unnecessary social institutions because clients are chosen for them without proper regard to responsive targeting. This is important when considering the variety of clients that halfway houses intend to service. Older offenders, for example, require different services than younger clients do. Race and ethnicity issues, gender issues, and other issues are ill-suited to be addressed by most current programs, which provide minimal meaningful assistance.

The halfway house solution to the problem of prisoner reentry may be referred to as a "halfway solution." This is appropriate, as the halfway house solution is also "half-price." A recent Ohio study (Lowenkamp, Latessa, & Smith, 2006) indicated that costs are higher for maintaining inmates in prisons as compared with halfway houses. This is good, in the sense that it offers a median between straight parole and incarceration. However, the phrase "you get what you pay for" can be applied to the mentality associated with the halfway house. Clients may be required to spend periods of time at halfway houses that are understaffed or underfunded. The more refined concept of intervention, which involves targeting relevant offenders with responsive programming, is not likely to be a financial reality anytime soon.

The most critical problem with halfway houses revolves around the limited set of services that are appropriate in a screening and targeting situation. To the extent that halfway houses can succeed in reforming their clientele with standardized program evaluations raises questions about best practices in rehabilitation. Yet, because of the political atmosphere, halfway houses are limited in their staffing capabilities.

Unfortunately, any effort to improve staffing at halfway houses to the optimum will cost a great deal more than prison. This is a quagmire that cannot be overcome.

Client-based intervention costs money, which is likely to make it politically unpopular. Current programs in halfway houses are not geared toward the needs of the people that reside in them, but politicians who run on platforms of crime control and seek solutions to the problem of recidivism with minimal financial incursion. It behooves politicians to argue for both long sentences and speak out against progressive programs such as halfway houses. Ironically, while the general public shows support for the tax incentives that accompany deinstitutionalization (Gray, Conover, & Hennessey, 1978), negative community reaction to transitional housing is almost a given (Piat,2000b). Communities support deinstitutionalization economically and philosophically, but take exception to both real and perceived negative community impacts such as diminished housing values and heightened crime rates (Kim, 2000). Often halfway house programs become politicized and it becomes difficult to empirically assess program success. Yet, there is much good intervention that is multi-modal. Because of political realities, halfway house programs have probably not been meeting their targets.

To highlight the matter of social necessity, there is the issue of impractical financial expenditures. Services delivered by halfway houses have simply not warranted evidence of a fiscally based argument. Alternatively, proponents of halfway houses express the importance of social justice, which might suggest that halfway houses are humane alternatives to either straight parole or incarceration. Although this is not a certainty, there is the suggestion that somehow the halfway house transcends mere economics. We admit to a degree that this is true. However, consider the following proposition: is social justice not served by spending tax money on improving minority relations or other infrastructural problems? We contend that one of the primary goals of social justice should be focusing on the greatest good for society in terms of public safety.

The nature of the association between fiscal expenditure and half-way houses is obvious. However, if it was the halfway house setting itself that provided the motivation for the Cheshire incident, any discussion of social justice being served by halfway houses remains moot. If the halfway house provided a networking opportunity for Hayes and Komisarjevsky, then such places should be considered affronts to social justice.

The alternatives of straight parole or simple extended incarceration can be seen as much more humane in this light. One alternative to community-based halfway houses was seriously considered at a 2008 U.S. Congressional hearing, when committee members discussed the possibility of building new halfway houses on the grounds of existing prisons (La Vigne 2010). We must question both the financial and social justice ramifications of continuing to support the halfway house as a social institution.

CHAPTER 5

THE GREATER GOOD

WHY WE NEED HALFWAY HOUSES

Although a conservative view of correctional thinking appears to dominate public discourse and the simple philosophy of "lock them up" may seem politically popular, in actuality, Roberts (1998) cited public opinion surveys that clearly state support for rehabilitation and effective community corrections. The primary idea is that people support rehabilitation as long as they have faith that the program is well-run and uses tax dollars efficiently. The public might be outraged if the program spends too much money or if it is ineffective.

There are no simple arguments supporting the drug treatment and rehabilitation of ex-convicts that halfway houses most often perform. Treatment for substance abusers reduces crime (Gossop et al., 2005). Treatment compliance leads to lower levels of violent behavior (Swartz et al., 1998) and, in the case of the criminal halfway house, often helps ex-convicts find vocations that keep them out of further trouble. In the case of substance-abuse halfway houses, they can serve a dual purpose, benefiting both the drug user and the ex-convict resident. Once an individual ceases being drug dependent, learns a vocation, or earns a GED, it is less likely that that person will turn to crime to support their lifestyle. A vicious cycle of "getting high" often makes drug users less employable as the need for money accrues through addiction costs. (Bennett & Wright, 2006). Therefore, many addicts turn to criminal behavior to support their habits when they are not incarcerated or in treatment (Ball et al., 1983).

Short-term pharmacological or behavioral treatment is certainly more cost-effective than residential housing (Shepard et al., 1999). People often receive short-term intervention in the initial phases of treatment, which stalls out in a few months or years. For governments, medical institutions, or anyone else addressing the problem, an outpatient pharmacological treatment such as methadone maintenance provides a cheaper solution to the problem of addiction than long-term residential treatment does. Additionally, straight parole, which involves no provision of social services, allows probationary officials to assign massive caseloads to only a few officers. A significant number of discharged prisoners (Metraux & Culhane, 2004), as well as a number of individuals discharged from psychiatric hospitals (Kuno et al., 2000), rely on shelters as a last resort for a place to stay. Although many programs are poor quality, the simple hope of having a warm place to sleep can provide a bit of hope for individuals seeking rehabilitation and recovery. However, such simple treatment may not produce the best long-term results for either addicts or ex-convicts.

One of the reasons that this book is necessary is to examine the notion that short-term treatment works. We seek to point out many myths about treatment, as well as debunking the idea that quantitative research can solve the myriad problems faced by habitual drug abusers. There are, of course, many methodological barriers to measuring success in the cases of both addiction problems and ex-convict reform. In the case of addiction problems, one of the most common methods for measuring treatment success is abstinence from drugs over a period of time (Doran, 2008). Such studies are inherently flawed because it is so difficult to measure the success of a treatment program. Similarly, Walters (2000) suggested that the questions involved in studying addiction are primarily qualitative. By contrast, quantitative studies often neglect to measure the contributions to society that rehabilitation might bring about, such as reduced criminality through expanded drug treatment or long-term residential programs.

Many studies of rehabilitation are similarly flawed because they ignore the interplay between substance abuse, mental health, and criminality issues. For example, a researcher attempting to explore the efficiency of halfway houses might use successful employment upon completion as a measure of success. However, although halfway houses might appear to have immediately reformed an ex-convict or addict who becomes employed during and after a residential stay, there can still be uncured problems with addiction that will pop up in the future. Thus, we feel that most quantitative studies of halfway houses have very little validity.

Quantitative studies of halfway house effectiveness show no standard methodology. In other words, they often lack a standardized way to show that halfway houses are successful. This book, in part, is an attempt to overcome some of those methodological failures through intensive qualitative research. That being said, most statistical analyses of halfway houses tend to show mixed results. As Lowenkamp, Latessa, and Holsinger (2006) stated: "for residential and nonresidential programs, adhering to the risk principle has a strong relationship with a program's ability to reduce recidivism" (p. 77). Quite simply, the individual program does not recover, the individual does. The house only offers a safe environment where people receiving assistance may work on their rehabilitation. With the lack of any definitive research on halfway houses in commissioned reports and peer-reviewed literature, the quest for answers becomes difficult. Some have suggested that prisons, or extended prison stays, should replace the halfway house for ex-convicts. Others have suggested that straight parole is a solution that would be less expensive but still result in the same inevitable outcome. For people on drugs, there is also no direct evidence that the assistance of halfway houses is any more or less effective than going "cold turkey." And, of course, there is always the matter of social justice to be concerned about. Solutions such as straight parole or expecting an addict to go cold turkey might prove to be less expensive than halfway houses. However, whether or not such solutions are conducive to any moral high ground remains a gray area.

PRISONS ARE NOT THE ANSWER

There are numerous problems with today's prison system that make it virtually impossible for modern prisons to claim any credit at all in terms of prison rehabilitation. The latest Bureau of Justice statistics and explorations into American prisons show that they are overcrowded, rife with gangs and violence, plagued by problems of sexual assaults, and that they have trouble retaining qualified staff members. To argue that prisons offer a more sophisticated tool for reform than community-based reform would be futile. However, we agree that prison is a suitable place for some people—specifically, known violent criminals who rape and murder such as Hayes and Komisarjevsky. For the majority of others who find themselves in an American prison today, we seek to explore the possibility of residencies in halfway houses both as potential aids in reform as well as full-blown punishments for minor crimes. We discuss this idea in more detail below.

In 1981, David Bellis wrote (p. 169), "After the state of California spends more than $20,000 a year for each inmate at CRC, he is given about $100 at the gate and told to go home and report to his parole agent. *Go home to what?*"

Multiple failures related to direct community release following incarceration or treatment make a case for the exploration of aftercare programs. Although these programs are abundant in the United States, there is a substantial lack of uniformity in how these programs operate. There are numerous ways to define populations that each group serves. One house might seek to take a certain type of offender from prisons, whereas other houses may seek residents that are substance abusers but lack criminal records. Other homes may specialize in psychiatric treatment. In many cases, it is difficult to isolate the problem without acknowledging that many prisoners have mental health and/or substance abuse problems. Similarly, many substance abusers might have broken laws at some time during their substance-abusing career. Because of this, we modify our definition of the halfway house slightly to meet a specific criteria put forth by Harry Allen and others (1978). Halfway houses can be viewed as "institutions that provide residential services to adult offenders as a transitional step between their release from an institution and their return to independent living within the community."

Of course, this catch-all definition might offend many people. There is a substantial stigma associated with placing the mentally ill in the same category as criminals. However, in terms of community response, any house with a substantial population of members of any of these groups is seen as undesirable neighbors by most people.

Community-based corrections, a category that includes things such as electronic monitoring, community service, and residential treatment programs, has consistently grown over the last fifty years. For the last fifty years, many have argued that prisons are ineffective at rehabilitating the offender (Martinson, 1974). Allen et al. (1978) argued that community-based corrections are important for three reasons. First, community-based correctional methods are more humane than traditional penal institutions. Second, they are better at reintegrating the offender into the community. Finally, they can operate more cost-effectively than a traditional prison can.

Under the laws of most states, offenders can be sentenced to a residential treatment program for up to two years either after their release from jail or prison or as an alternative to jail or prison. Some judges place offenders in treatment centers as a condition of pretrial release. In California, residential treatment programs are often a component of Drug Court programs in lieu of regular probation. Failure to complete the treatment usually results in a jail sentence.

The crack cocaine epidemic and increased enforcement of laws prohibiting drunk driving have motivated some states to reprioritize their community corrections strategies. Some states (such as Texas, Michigan, Florida, South Carolina, and Oregon) have made drug and alcohol treatment a major component of their community corrections sanctions.

First-time offenders must undergo varying degrees of risk assessment prior to sentencing to determine the required level of supervision and the intensity of drug or alcohol treatment. Repeat offenders who are sentenced to jail or prison must also be assessed and could be eligible for further treatment inside the jail or prison system.

There are some studies (Belenko & Peugh,2005) that show that such treatment programs work well when they are part of an overall court sentence. Belenko's (2005) study indicates that the longer an offender remains in and completes a treatment program (more than 3 months), the less the likelihood of recidivism. Studies of drug and alcohol treatment programs in Oregon and Michigan show similar results: they led to reduced jail and probation and a reduction in future criminal arrests and convictions.

However, although it is likely that the increased possibility of using halfway houses as criminal sentences will cause tension among community residents, we argue that many of them do benefit society as a whole. Both criminal halfway houses and substance abuse halfway houses have proved to be effective, but only when there is a principle of response of treatment involved.

There are numerous ways to treat various types of substance abusers. Some of these ways are more effective than others. It is necessary to have a person in residential treatment to figure out what kind of addict he or she is. Substance abuse problems do exist, and not just among street-level junkies. As is the case with many of the people we interviewed, such as Sean and Bernard, college experience proved to be a catalyst for further drug experience. Many colleges probably have substance abuse problems.

The college population consists of young, curious individuals who have significant amounts of time that is unstructured. Many universities have relatively low-cost housing in the immediate area. It would be ridiculous to assume that each and every college student in a town gets investigated or arrested for drugs. When a former student was asked about his drug use and parties in the area throughout his college career, he claimed that unless someone did something egregious, college students are usually "let go" by the police as long as the neighbors don't complain about noise. This student went on to joke about how many college students would be arrested if every police department in America decided to "search all the dorms at once." (Personal interview: Steve, a college student)

As with substance abuse, criminal halfway houses are a good idea because long-term contact with qualified staff adds to the effectiveness of rehabilitative reform. Each criminal offender has a unique set of characteristics. Some are driven to offense by addiction, whereas others have deeper problems that come from childhoods of abuse. Because parole and prisons mainly focus on keeping offenders in line, one would be hard-pressed to find a situation in which either parole or prison contributed to a genuine reform.

Again, it is important to specify the therapeutic nature of the halfway house and the importance of the practitioner in the clinical situation, regardless of whether the halfway house focuses on criminals, drug addicts, or mentally unstable individuals. Weider (p. 47–48, 1988) illustrated five significant points made by practitioners about halfway houses:

1. The first thirty to sixty days after a man has been released from prison are judged by correctional workers to be the most difficult.
2. The halfway house is proposed as a device for helping the ex-prisoner make the terrible and risky transition from captivity to freedom.
3. The halfway house is described as a "normal" or "home-like" environment.
4. The halfway house is portrayed as a short-term arrangement where quickly increasing responsibilities are placed on the ex-prisoner and he quickly becomes ready to fully rely on his own efforts.
5. The new parolee is portrayed as experiencing severe anxiety and frustration in his initial sojourns into the free world. (Wieder 1988)

During our interviews, we interviewed several practitioners who offered valid qualifications of these arguments. When asked about the effectiveness of Salvation City's halfway house programs, Andrew discussed the neighborhood that the majority of Salvation City's halfway house programs are located in and pointed out that they are not conducive to criminal activity.

> I can understand people that don't have a working knowledge of the halfway house to be intimidated by some of these folks. But look at the assault rate in town. Look at the burglaries. Look at the armed robbery. It's non-existent.
>
> (Personal interview: Andrew)

Much of this statement makes sense from a therapeutic standpoint. People in recovery or in community release are less likely to focus on their own program if they are exposed to too many influences outside the program. Therefore, in Salvation City, there is not really a counterargument for someone to wake up, go to work, return to the house, and go to a twelve-step meeting before returning to the home for the night.

The major drawback to using correctional warehousing as a response to crime is that prisons are geared toward punishment and not rehabilitation. Even minimum-security prisons often act as warehouses that offer no viable rehabilitative programs. The most common form of rehabilitative program offered by today's prisons is a simple GED program, and the majority of American prisons appear to be unwilling to build a concept of vocational or educational training that exceeds that scope.

To make matters worse, America has, since the 1980s, been in the midst of what is known as the "penal harm" movement, a commonly shared philosophy that prisons should operate to harm the individual as much as possible. Therefore if someone is beaten up, raped, or left without proper nutrition or medical supplies, there is a new movement emerging that justifies it. (For a detailed history of the penal harm movement, see: Cullen, 1995) We are overstating the political rhetoric of reactionary politicians here, but one might say a philosophy that is popular in America for many voters is "Do the crime, do the time!"

Prisoners today, as compared with prisoners of fifty years ago, find themselves in an exceedingly different situation. Financially, America is struggling. This makes it easier to overlook the wellbeing of its prisoners. Prison reform is simply not a topic of discourse among politicians anymore. Today's prisoners are stuck in warehouses and there are very few trained professionals who care about reform efforts. The sole purpose of most prisons has become punishment. As advocates of community corrections, this leaves us in a difficult position. The emphasis on punishment in prison leaves very few qualified individuals in a position to ensure that an addict becomes sober or whether an illiterate person learns to read. It is perhaps better if some convicts are treated through community correctional programs, such as halfway houses, because we feel that it is in some convicted persons' and societies' best interests. Prisons are clearly not the answer because their focus is not on reform, but punishment. To make matters worse, due to all the fighting and gang-related activity that is reported as a staple of prison life, it is often possible that people who are convicted and imprisoned on minor, nonviolent charges leave prison as violence-oriented criminals.

Unfortunately, although many people being treated in today's halfway house programs have never been in a prison situation, many members of the undiscerning public view them as hardened criminals.

Among the people we interviewed, there was no tendency for people to distinguish between addicted or criminal halfway house residents in their neighborhood. However, although we suggest that labeling is an important factor in reform, how the surrounding community views the halfway house resident is probably less important than the actual treatment provided inside.

Although creating model citizens with high-paying jobs, encouraging complete sobriety, and preventing all criminal behavior is the ideal, it is doubtful that the halfway house can ever achieve it. However, even halfway house programs based on harm reduction (a model stressing gradual cessation from substance abuse or crime) are better than prison-based alternatives. There are many other staples of prison life, such as factory work, that are not intended to better the condition of the prisoner. Rather, they are intended to help the prison meet financial needs. One example that is often mentioned in conversations about the Louisiana prison system is the Rodeo at Angola, a tourist attraction which has gone on for almost half a century. Such programs may be fun for the public, but they do not provide any real assistance to reform efforts.

There are many statistics that confirm that prisons are also not the best place for people to reform. Recent BJS (Bureau of Justice Statistics) indicate that one out of every six people will die in prison, either by natural death or of a homicide or suicide. There have been further estimates that 90 percent of all prisoners will be physically assaulted in prison, and Human Rights Watch indicated that anywhere from 20 to 60 percent of male prisoners will be sexually assaulted either by staff members or other inmates (Mariner, 2001).

Community corrections are, in general, conducive to lower risk behavior. We argue that community corrections are better than the alternative of life in prison for many offenders. Although we agree that there are many who belong in prison for life, such as those who murder or rape, we feel that prison with all of its problems is not a suitable place to rehabilitate or reform a person in the modern age. We look at prisons and see a portrait of a gang-controlled, overcrowded environment with inadequate staff and a strong underground economy that is based on the exchange of everything from cigarettes to Twinkies (Kalinich & Stojkovic, 1987).

In conclusion, one may point to statistical evidence and argue that people are no less likely to recidivate whether they exit prison on straight parole or via a halfway house. To this idea we offer a counterargument that is steeped in moral justification. If we are going to send people to a place as inhumane as prison, then we should at least let them exit via a humane path.

PSYCHIATRIC TREATMENT IS NOT THE ANSWER

One individual, Jane, whose experience was detailed in our case studies for this book, spent a great deal of time in a place that she sarcastically called the "Nut Hatch." (Personal interview: Jane) This was a slang term for the mental institution that she was placed in after her first and second overdoses. She complained about being overmedicated, treated poorly, and about the ineffectiveness of the hospital placement protocol. Although we feel that she might have been exaggerating in some points, we do not feel that she was completely wrong when she emphasized some of the shortcomings of hospitals and mental institutions. We are especially concerned about high comments that such places may place emphasis on the medicinal treatment of people who may be inappropriately diagnosed. Classic research indicates that people who are subject to institutional mental health treatment experience feelings of dehumanization from several aspects of hospital life (Szasz, 1970). In many hospitals, there are also known misclassification problems that result in a uniform treatment of all psychiatric patients from manic-depressives to drug addicts (Rosenhan, 1973).

Jane's problems were brought on by an entire lifetime of mistreatment at the hands of her mother and then her foster family. Yet, the hospital attempted to treat her with quick-fix medications. She also reported feeling dehumanized by several aspects of hospital life. For example, her experience of being told to fill out questionnaires after she attempted suicide falls in line with many people's complaints about hospitalization being a "one directional" and assuming treatment process (Rosenhan, 1973). Upon hearing her case, we could not help but notice that many American prisons' problems are shared by psychiatric treatment facilities. In Jane's interview, she reported that the hospital was overcrowded. In the psychiatric treatment program, she said that manic-depressives and drug addicts were housed together, put in the same "talk groups" together, and told not to help one another. American prisons encounter a similar problem when jails are so overcrowded that drug dealers have to be placed in the same cells or cellblocks as rapists or murderers.

Jane also reported having to "sleep on the floor" because there were no beds available for her. This (the shortage of supplies and available space) is also a problem with American prisons. Jane also pointed out issues with staff members who "backstabbed" her and took a punitive or patronizing approach toward her detoxification stay.

What was eventually necessary in Jane's case to help her get on the "road to recovery" was a "humanizing experience." The psychiatric hospital offered the exact opposite, ironically. It is obvious that treatment one-on-one with a counselor who could understand her motives worked better than did several high-tech medications.

We also believe that Jane's experience of being clustered with manic-depressives and other psychiatric patients was not unique. It is a true dysfunction in American psychiatric hospitals that acts as the proverbial "elephant in the living room" when discussing current psychiatric care. One's first reaction upon seeing a hospital treatment group filled with manic-depressives and substance abusers would probably be "Why are they together? They don't have the same problem." This grouping of dissimilar patients together is consistent with what Goffman wrote about in his 1961 sociological classic *Asylums*.

However, for a psychiatric hospital, the grouping of such patients together can be justified using an old psychoanalytic model of psychology which views drug use as a simple symptom of mental illness. Of course, the reality is that many hospitals seek to streamline patient care in order to maximize revenue.

There are harsh realities related to mental illness discussed by the President's New Freedom Commission on Mental Health, a group that was commissioned by George W. Bush to eliminate inequality for Americans with disabilities. Among the commission's concerns were the following:

1. Coordination of Care is necessary.
2. Barriers to Transportation are necessary to overcome.
3. Stigma and lack of support for community entry is necessary to overcome.

[Substance Abuse and Mental Health Services Administration, 2003]

We feel that well-run Residential Treatment Centers have more potential to meet these goals than today's psychiatric hospitals do.

COORDINATION OF CARE

For persons who require long periods of structured supervision and supportive therapy for substance abuse coupled with legal problems, a well-run halfway house can provide better-coordinated support than a psychiatric hospital run by patronizing staff can. Additionally, well-run centers provide supervision, specialized services, and access to legal services for felony and misdemeanor offenders with alcohol and drug dependencies, mental impairments, and emotional problems. Typically, one or more of these problem areas have contributed to the offender's criminal record, yet such problems remain unaddressed in a traditional psychiatric institution. In some halfway houses, staff regularly evaluate the offenders' behavior, attitude, and progress in relation to their legal situation. All evaluations are filed with the sentencing judge.

BARRIERS TO TRANSPORTATION SERVICES

Since a person in a halfway house is not committed to staying in one particular room all day, there is more emphasis on the person's need for transportation services than there is in a traditional psychiatric hospital setting.

An emphasis on persons' needs to be transported from point A to point B is prevalent in halfway houses. People in halfway houses, must have a way to get to work and the store for basic necessities Specifically, because halfway house residents usually have to pay some kind of rent on a sliding scale, they actually find it in their and the house's best interests to have access to transportation. Many of the halfway house residents we spoke to found it rewarding to have access to transportation. In many ways, some of these people indicated that the small bit of freedom that they achieved from being able to "get around" made them feel somewhat empowered and generally more healthy and normal.

STIGMA AND LACK OF SUPPORT FOR COMMUNITY ENTRY

In this book, we do not limit ourselves to the narrow-minded vision that all halfway houses will be successful. In fact, one of the principal reasons that we chose Salvation City as the idyllic place for halfway houses was because it was consistent with the tradition of charity and understanding. There are advantages for a cluster of recovery homes to develop in a certain area. Although one needs a location with access to a significant number of services to coordinate, there is additional efficiency in a small city because the people maintaining support systems and social services are likely to know each other better than in cities with large operations and numerous case workers. They can share information in a much more efficient manner.

To some degree, the efficiency with which information is shared ties into the first proposition mentioned earlier about coordination of care. However, it is also known that many small towns lack support for community reentry. If halfway houses are to exist as a staple of community corrections, then the sharing of knowledge regarding the halfway house and its presence in the community must be something that is addressed with some prudence.

To put it bluntly, halfway houses cannot work as functional reform facilities in neighborhoods where they do not receive support. This is because the reentry process carries with it a great deal of stigma for each individual. Takahashl (1997) described the three phases of stigma: non-productivity, dangerousness, and personal culpability. Primary concerns are non-productivity and lack of functionality among the residents. Being seen out on the porch smoking during the day when most people are working feeds these perceptions. The perception of dangerousness is fed by media reports about horrible incidents such as the Petit invasion.

WHY WE NEED HALFWAY HOUSES

In the beginning of this book, we indicated that we were concerned about moral and social justice. We are concerned about these things not just for offenders but for communities as well. We realize that the idea of having a halfway house in one's neighborhood can be quite unnerving to community residents. On the other hand, we feel that the houses provide invaluable service to those communities in the long run by reforming the prisoners. Home invasions, such as the Cheshire incident, are so rare that it is hard to not think that the needs of the many outweigh the needs of the few. We feel that despite the mixed results in previous research, halfway houses can work and they are uniquely more important than psychiatric hospitals, prisons, and even straight parole with intensive supervision. Our interviews have given us much insight into what is necessary to make halfway houses successful, which we discuss in the conclusion to this book.

We feel that it is necessary that halfway houses, and the proprietors of those houses, continue to perform their function with due diligence even if facing community adversity. Assuming halfway houses had sufficient funding to develop ideal programs, it would be most difficult to launch a public relations campaign for a halfway house. Such an effort might involve showing the residents of the halfway house performing public service, so that the publicity is positive rather than bad.

Chapter 6

Conclusions

We were led to one ultimate conclusion during our evaluation of halfway house programs: halfway houses and associated programs are necessary to help many individuals restore balance to their lives. We discovered that many individuals veer away from both criminal lifestyles and substance abuse issues within the confines of the halfway house. In well-programmed halfway houses, residents live under regulated conditions that are specifically designed to keep them away from contaminating influences: the bars, gang activity, drug connections, etc., that led them to the halfway house setting to begin with. In addition, we found that the restrictive environment of the halfway house tends to be an irritant for many triggers of criminal behavior. In criminal halfway houses, the residents we interviewed were unable to associate with former criminal associates. In substance-abuse halfway houses, the residents we interviewed were sequestered from possible triggers of using drugs and alcohol, such as abusive relationships.

We also came to understand that further empirical study of halfway houses must be qualitative. People needing transitional living arrangements often succeed in ways that are not measurable through quantitative research. A transitional living arrangement sometimes helps to facilitate an orderly state of mind that is not quantifiable. The halfway house as an impetus to get one's life in order was a common theme expressed by many of those we interviewed. In quantitative research, a successful halfway house treatment might be measured as abstinence from substance abuse, or it might be measured by desistance from crime for convicted people; however, quantitative studies of these measures have yielded mixed results.

We ascertained from our many interviews and experiences that halfway houses do work if they are well run and offer a chance for people to regain control of their lives. Whether certain halfway house programs offer hope or salvation can also be beyond the scope of quantitative research. Furthermore, how deeply families are affected by the halfway house situation may elude researchers. We also conclude that, due to the nature of confidentiality in medical care records and private records related to incarceration, achieving one single and reliable measure of the success of halfway house programming is virtually impossible. Multiple individual case studies need to be taken into account to further understand programming outcomes.

FACTORS AFFECTING HALFWAY HOUSE PROGRAMMING AND OUTCOMES

The primary problem that both criminal and substance-abuse halfway house programming efforts face can be summarized with a quick glance at opponents in the community. Although we address the NIMBY phenomenon throughout this book, we also feel that there are significant benefits to having halfway houses in certain communities. The debates about halfway houses' placement in communities revolve around the idea that the presence of a halfway house decreases community safety (Krause, 1991). But, a worthy counterargument to this is that halfway houses improve the quality of life in a given area by attracting law enforcement and social service providers to that area.

Residents of neighborhoods we interviewed perceived themselves as greatly affected in terms of feeling their neighborhoods had been unjustly targeted for transitional residences (Cowan 2003). Many residents we interviewed felt down on their luck. When people recounted their experiences during interviews, we were touched by the feeling that they were very troubled about halfway houses in their neighborhoods. This is how we got to meet some of the local people that we interviewed in Salvation City. As we came to know the individuals who were upset about the placement of halfway houses in their communities, we also came to know that they were not angry radicals or hateful individuals. Many of these individuals we interviewed believed that they were taking care of their own property values and showing concern about the safety of their families and other neighborhood residents.

When we began our research, the citizens of Salvation City were split between two public goods. First, the need for reform provision being felt throughout the states in which we conducted this research. Second, and at the same time, the freedom to protect property values and reside in a desirable community, knowing that property values of homes located near halfway houses are likely to drop. We witnessed this in many local television newscasts and newspapers where transitional housing had become the center of controversy, and made a personal and professional decision to research the problem. At some level, we felt an obligation to the community to be problem solvers instead of just researchers. Both authors of this book extensively studied all aspects of the recovery process, including psychotherapeutic treatment, vocational treatment, twelve-step meetings, prayer groups, revival groups, hospital-run support groups, and educational training. As professors of behavioral science, former students of ours were employed in all of the above fields and they all took different approaches to the problem of criminal and drug rehabilitation. Some of the approaches were psychological, some more spiritual, others were military or disciplinary in nature— especially those efforts we witnessed at criminal halfway houses. We also participated in several stages of a commissioned research project on halfway houses that provided a foundation for institutional knowledge of the halfway house and acted as a catalyst for putting the institutional research and the case studies together.

We found that halfway houses are prone to resource failures when communities are not supportive. In Salvation City, many individuals called radio talk shows to protest, wrote into their city council, wrote newspaper editorial sections, and visited town hall meetings in efforts to resist halfway house placement within their communities. In the introductory chapter, we referred to an interview in which a young girl was frightened of the halfway houses being placed near her residence. So were her parents.

When people resist placement of the halfway houses in a given area, they are prone to move away from that area and suspend investment in that area. As is the case with public schools, such flight away from geographic regions can lead to a suffering tax base and limited economy. There is no question about it: when it comes to community service priorities, we noted that halfway houses are usually one of the last items on the town council's agenda.

In our research efforts, we found many proponents of criminal and substance abuse halfway houses who were very vocal about their concerns. These people included professionals in the corrections and recovery community who are interested in these battles and their implications for the allocation of finite resources. During our research effort, we found that many of these corrections and recovery professionals facilitated the busing of rehabilitation supporters to counter-protest placement of halfway houses. People came from out of town to attend town hall meetings and discuss how these halfway houses actually helped them in their recovery. However, most of the local residents remained hostile toward attempts at halfway house placement in their communities. They were quick to counter with statements like "If you like them so much, why don't you take them in your neighborhood?"

We found that, in general and as expected, local citizens did not like the presence of halfway houses. We also discovered that many residents' feelings about halfway houses escalated as more publicity was generated. As recognition of halfway house controversies was heightened, more resistance developed among the general populace. There is some consistency here with the early arguments of social construction-ists. Problems are real if we perceive them as such. Although we do not deny that halfway houses can create a danger for communities, we wonder how much of that danger is actually real, as opposed to merely perceived.

In summary, with regard to the halfway house placement issue and how it affects taxpayers' allocations, we noticed that the more protest we witnessed, the more prone that city councils were to filibustering spending on halfway house improvements. When states face budget cri-ses, departments of health, hospitals, and correctional departments face budget cuts. When cutting the budget, it is difficult to cut the prisons and hospitals that are already in operation. Therefore, block grants that funded halfway house operations that we observed were reduced. This reduction in correctional and medical spending affected halfway houses to the extent that they were forced into notable staff reductions. In some of the houses we studied, employee hours were reduced, professional counselors were streamlined out (in place of untrained and cheaper per-sonnel), and general repairs were neglected.

It is difficult to sell taxpayers on halfway houses at this point in our economic history. Cowan (2003) points out several ways that transitional residence officials and sponsors might attempt to appeal to community sentiment. That said, there are myriad reasons for both taxpayers and community residents to view transitional housing skeptically, these are:

1. There are few alternatives to the solution of the care provision problem
2. There are risks related to community release that are perhaps worse than the halfway houses in the area.
3. Community release for someone who is not ready to enter the community from continued incarceration or institutionalization does not address problems with integrity.

Likewise, such institutionalization is likely to be significantly more expensive and dangerous than halfway house programs. Institutionalization is expensive and it does not necessarily cure the problem of crime or sobriety. Releasing someone into the community before they are ready can lead to a risk of these individuals' continuing the behaviors that got them institutionalized in the first place.

One question that may be asked by the taxpayer is: "Is the average cost of keeping a prisoner in a traditional facility above the average cost of maintaining halfway houses?" In support of community-based correctional options, many have underscored the issue of limited government fiscal resources available to sustain support for populations in need (Gray, Conover & Hennessey, 1978; Jones, 1991; Petersilia, 1995). Transitional residence facilities have occasionally been demonstrated as a cost-effective way of dealing with substance abuse, mental health and/ or correctional populations.

Perhaps the most important discovery during our research and interviews was that there are a series of problems to be addressed in the programming of halfway houses.

FACILITATING THE GREAT GOOD: WHICH DIRECTION NEXT?

The problem of limited resources in dealing with increasing numbers of individuals on probation suggests a need for more community supervision (Latessa, 2004). Among these existing forms of community supervision are halfway houses, which represent a community-based effort to facilitate offender reentry and substance abuse rehabilitation.

As sociologists, we are concerned with the operations of halfway houses because of their implications for social justice and the community. On a socioeconomic level, we are concerned with their financial expenditures and sources of income, as these houses are usually placed in lower-status areas. At the criminological level, we are concerned with the rehabilitation of people residing in halfway houses and their relationships to the neighbors around them. At the organizational level, we are concerned about interactions among the professionals that work in halfway houses. Finally, as a political matter, we are concerned with interactions among competing social groups regarding the placement of halfway houses. At all levels, of course, we are concerned with tangible programming outcomes.

However, all of the above concerns are only ancillary to our primary concern, which we stated earlier as "the greater good." In many ways, this book addresses the question of the greater good in community sociology.

Are halfway houses helpful for substance abusers?

According to our research and that of many others, halfway houses do indeed help people with addiction problems (Hitchcock et al., 1995; Jason, 2001).

Are halfway houses helpful to rehabilitating criminal offenders?

Our research says that they can be, as referenced earlier in Luis's case. Mixed results have emerged from several other empirical studies (Lowenkamp & Latessa, 2005; Lowenkamp, Latessa, & Smith, 2006; Sigler & Lamb, 1995).

How do halfway houses affect the mentality of residents within areas?

Our research tells us that they have a negative effect on community morale. We interviewed many residents who strongly opposed the state approval of halfway house placements in their neighborhood. Many of the residents we interviewed felt victimized by the state. Some were concerned with their immediate safety, whereas others were upset about the reality of property values declining. Our findings follow Piat (2000a), Johnson (2006), and Schively (2007), who also pointed out the highly emotional responses among community residents.

Are halfway houses worthy of continual funding from the state?

We find that they are absolutely necessary. The benefits of rehabilitating individual substance abusers or criminals save the costs of incarceration and creates tax-paying citizens. Rehabilitation eases the burden of long-suffering family members who care for relatives with criminal records or substance abuse issues. The research that we gathered demonstrates that halfway houses are underfunded. One resident we interviewed pointed out: "The stairwells smell like piss because there isn't enough bathroom space for all the house residents. I swear I'm going to start sleeping with a bucket in my room at night." (Personal interview: Will)

All of these questions speak to our moral sensibilities. We recognize the need to reconcile communities with halfway houses as both a practical and a financial matter. At the same time, we recognize the problem as a public health issue. Aggregates of people who are geographically clustered and perceive themselves as victims may become morally cynical. In turn, this affects their quality of life.

We feel that one of the ways to address this perceived inequity is to focus on the potential good that halfway houses can provide to communities. But, in order to achieve a stasis between the halfway house and the community that surrounds it, it is necessary that halfway houses be run with enough integrity to earn the respect of community members. We recognize that halfway houses' abilities to rehabilitate residents is often contingent upon the quality of programming they offer. With this in mind, we note several observations with regard to best practices in halfway house programming.

Rossi (1978, p. 577) claimed that "the establishment of a human services delivery system rests upon a number of critical assumptions, as follows:

1. There are deficient individuals, households, or institutional arrangements. These deficiencies prevent optimal functioning of some individuals and households. Furthermore, the presence of these individual and / or institutional deficiencies in the society presents problems to the society.
2. If the deficiencies can be corrected or compensated for, functioning can be changed so that individuals and households can function "normally" through the use of some sort of human service "treatment."

3. The human services "treatment" can be delivered uniformly and widely through the training of delivery personnel and through the placement of them in the organization.

4. There are no serious conflicts of interests between the social control goals of human services and the goals of clients."

As Rossl specified, points two and three are critical to rehabilitative success. There is something to be said about well-run halfway houses and their degree of programming integrity. With regard to criminal halfway houses, Lowenkamp, Latessa, and Smith (2006) claimed that the quality of a program is an essential factor in reducing recidivism. This may be due to the intensive nature of supervision that halfway house residents are subjected to during the early months of parole. Parole officers frequent most halfway houses and some are monitored around the clock. In this sense, we find the halfway house to be an effective tool for preventing recidivism early on.

BEST PRACTICES: RESPONSIVITY AND QUALITY OF SERVICE

The responsivity principle (Andrews et al., 1990) is the idea that interpersonal relationships between staff and inmates within the confines of a correctional institution need to target the specific modality of treatment charged to the specific need of the inmate. As we observed in many cases, those staff members showing more empathy and sensitivity toward a client's needs will build stronger relationships and have greater impact upon the reform process. Such was the case when we interviewed Jane, who indicated that her affinity for and attachment to her counselor greatly helped with the rehabilitative process. In short, applied to the halfway house, the responsivity principle means that halfway house residents need a modality of treatment tailored to their needs.

How can we tell if a halfway house program is run with integrity?

One the most commonly accepted methods of measuring program integrity is the Correctional Programming Assessment Inventory (CPAI),

FIGURE **6.1.** Measuring Correctional Integrity.

Institutional integrity	Has the need for the program been empirically documented? Are programs based on credible scientific evidence?
Client pre-service assessment	Does the client have a history of substance abuse and peer association?
Program implementation	Does an agency have a history of adopting new initiatives? Is there task or emotional-personal conflict within the organization at the interdepartmental, staff, management, and/or management-staff levels?
Staff characteristics	Does the change agent have an intimate knowledge of the agency and its staff? Does the change agent have the support of senior agency officials as well as that of line staff? Do the staff members follow the institutional rules?
Outcome analysis	The CPAI considers prevention and aftercare to assess how the program reroutes offenders to the community.
Miscellaneous	The CPAI considers the transitional theme of finding family and community resources.

developed by Gendreau and Andrews in 1989. Because each halfway house differs in terms of its selection of residents, staffing, programs, and financing (Carpenter, 1978), they should be assessed accordingly. The CPAI measures six main factors with regard to institutional integrity: program implementation, client pre-service assessment, program characteristics, staff characteristics, outcome evaluation, and miscellaneous factors. There are 66 items contained within the CPAI to assess responsive intervention (Matthews, Jones-Hubbard, & Latessa, 2001). The total score of any given correctional program yields a rating of "very satisfactory" (70% to 100%), "satisfactory" (60% to 69%), "satisfactory, but needs improvement" (50% to 59%), or "unsatisfactory" (less than 50%). Figure 6.1 provides the reader with some examples that are taken into account in the CPAI in each category.

Along these lines, Lowenkamp, Latessa, and Holsinger (2006) used the CPAI in an evaluation of Ohio halfway houses. The researchers found that failures in program integrity were significant predictors of offenders' readmission to prisons for new crimes. Likewise, research by Bonta et al. (2008) showed that halfway houses with lower success rates had a lack of staff integrity and were also plagued by probation and parole officers who spent too much time on the enforcement aspect of supervision and not enough time on the service-delivery role. From our interviews with people who had criminal records, such as Luis and Bernard, it was also suggested that probation and parole officers sometimes might lack the necessary skills to influence behavioral change in their clients

The CPAI is a very helpful tool in assessing best practices. It is, we feel, one of the ways to mend the schism between halfway houses and communities and to facilitate the greater good. However, the CPAI does not offer a complete picture of the quality of services offered. The inventory is a bureaucratic checklist. What is needed to determine best practices in a valid way is an assessment that takes into account not only the halfway house, but also the more nuanced quality of relationships between the facility and the community that surrounds it. It is granted that part of the CPAI is designated to look at community resources. However, it focuses on the community from the perspective of the institution.

One idea that can be expanded upon is the nature of evaluation of halfway houses. Allen et al. (1994) suggested that there are seven issues that must be covered during programming evaluation:

1. Assessment of need and setting goals and objectives.
2. Issues and problems of funding a halfway house.
3. Administration and organizational structure of the house.
4. The location and site selection for the house.
5. Issues involved in house programs and services.
6. Issues of standards for and accreditation of halfway houses.
7. Issues and problems of program evaluation.

VISION HOUSE

As a model of a well run a halfway house, we will take some time to explain the workings of Vision House in Salvation City. The house is located in a lower-income residential neighborhood. It is a well-kept facility. The exterior of the house is actually better-kept than many of the houses of the residents that surround it. It is funded by a series of state grants from both correctional and health departments and also by some charitable giving.

Brian, a resident of Vision House for five months, said that "Dr. Kramer saved my life." Dr. Kramer was the individual who started Vision House. It began when he was providing indigent health care. He noticed that many individuals who had criminal records and were being treated for substance abuse needed more than simple doctor visits. He met with social workers and other neighboring health professionals in the field and began to turn his vision into reality.

Brian, who was convicted of negligent vehicular homicide during the late 1970s, had previously lived his life in a chemically induced haze. He grew up in an upper-middle-class childhood, which provided him with certain social skills that many ex-convicts do not have. He went to an elite preparatory school before he started college. He was drunk and on a date when he was arrested and convicted of the crime. His mother was frequently frustrated, wondering why he made one bad decision after another. She and his father worked very hard to provide opportunities for his advancement. He was very educated and articulate; however, at times during our interview he became surly and was frequently argumentative. The gothic inkwork of his tattoos, in addition to an unfinished prison tattoo (a self-portrait), belied his upbringing. He spoke with us about his experiences at Vision House with more carefully articulated thoughts than we got from many of our previous interviewees.

He had been incarcerated during the early 1980s. Shortly after leaving prison, he developed a janitorial service that made him wealthy. As his business success increased, Brian returned to drinking and substance abuse, which led to a series of problems. After losing his business, Brian found out that he needed a new liver. With all of his difficulties, Brian was likely facing death. Homeless and going to Dr. Kramer's clinic, Brian took one last chance at saving his life at Vision House. "It was my only hope and it got me back on my feet," Brian said. "I owe them my life." Ironically, Brian commented that Salvation City had "too many halfway houses" and that he was "lucky he found the right one." He said, "How's an individual supposed to get recovery when they don't have a job? There're a bunch of people in my position. There's a lot of the losers who can't get on their feet. I don't think that I deserve help more than them, but I do think I got that." (Personal interview: Brian)

We noted other things about Vision House that fit in well with the requirements of the CPAI. For example, while the CPAI stipulates that house directors should hold at least a baccalaureate degree, Dr. Kramer was a qualified medical doctor. Because much of the money for the house came from the community, the program was very compliant and provided a significant amount of evidence for a pattern of effectiveness and responsible service delivery. According to Brian, Vision House adopted new programs quickly and was very quick to experiment with psychiatric medications when necessary. This is an institution that would have scored very high on the CPAI.

However, there were many subtleties behind the scenes regarding the establishment of Vision House that would have gone unnoted by the CPAI. One key element that the CPAI would not have measured was the informal interaction between Dr. Kramer and the community before establishing the house. When Dr. Kramer began Vision House, he got the consensual agreement of the community and the OK to build a halfway house in the neighborhood. He was not perceived as an outsider by the community, as many halfway house providers are. In designing the board of directors, he drew from compassionate residents in the community. These members of the board were longtime residents of the city and well known in the community as altruistic. Among them were people who were well known in local churches and respected by the community. In addition, Dr. Kramer, being deeply enmeshed with the Salvation City social service provision landscape, had connections at all levels of the rehabilitative process. These included connections with criminal justice professionals, health-care workers, and social workers that made the rehabilitation process smooth for residents.

In sum, we feel that one of the ways of making halfway houses accepted within communities is periodic assessment of their integrity. There are many tools to do this, including the CPAI. However, our ultimate recommendation is that the assessment of the greater good cannot be accomplished by a mere bureaucratic instrument. We support this statement by reiterating that the CPAI could not have noticed the subtleties of Dr. Kramer's interactions with the community before the establishment of Vision House.

As community sociologists, we could not help but focus on the intricacies of Kramer's social network. During our research, we noticed that a prevalent moral panic spread throughout communities just prior to the establishment of halfway houses. A person who is seen as a good citizen in the community, and not an outsider, will often provide the impetus for establishing an "institution that cares," and act as a mediator to ensure the transitional residence is run with integrity (personal interview: Dr. Kramer). In addition and more importantly, the CPAI does not focus on the history of the institution or the community. Therefore, although it is an adequate measure of programming integrity, it is simply not holistic enough. To understand halfway houses and their relationship to the greater good, it is necessary to understand the communities around them and the community spirit that prevails.

BALANCING ACT: COMMUNITY NEEDS VERSUS HALFWAY HOUSES

As community sociologists, we seek ways to put our work into practice to facilitate the greater good. Before we "discovered" Salvation City, our original title for this book was to be "Halfway houses: how they harm America's communities and why we need them." In discussion of the impact of social services on society as a whole, we again defer to Peter RossI (1978), who described the dilemma of the social minima and the societal minimum. Facilitating the greater good means facilitating both community residents and people seeking reform. The societal minimum acknowledges that the unemployed, the unrehabilitated, and those debilitated by substance abuse do not contribute to the welfare of others in the larger society. To some extent, this idea implies that residents of halfway houses have a negative effect on the utilitarian environment of the communities that surround them. We certainly feel that this is the case. Because halfway houses are becoming increasingly used for punishment, this issue will evolve into a major one in the United States.

At some levels, because quality of life is largely perceived according to one's immediate surroundings, the problem of the greater good and the halfway house can be viewed as a geographic matter. So, at some level, it is important to revisit the concept of NIMBY in regard to the greater good. Communities support deinstitutionalization economically and philosophically, but take exception to both real and perceived negative community impacts such as diminished housing values and heightened crime rates (Kim, 2000). While such transitional facilities simultaneously represent state-sponsored efforts toward easing taxpayer burdens and rehabilitation, communities often poorly react to the placement of such facilities (Orndoff,1978; Piat, 2000a).

As discussed throughout the text, the term NIMBY is frequently used to describe a social phenomenon in which many people support the services provided by the government, but they do not want the services located in their neighborhood. "Not In My Back Yard" has a rich and growing literature (Wilton, 2002; Cowan, 2003). The designated placement of transitional housing observed in this book is a matter that taps into many social justice core issues. Humans have inherent rights to fair wages, medical care, economic protection, decent education and specifically relevant here, a decent home in an environment free of classism.

Warren (2001) addressed the idea of consensual democracy as a key factor in maintaining the perceived well-being of a community, thus facilitating the greater good. The integrity of an institution within a community greatly influences both approval and denial regarding the siting of community care institutions (Matejczyk, 2001). Consensual democracy is a concept that relates to community empowerment and perceived victimization. The central idea in discovering that the greater good relies heavily on such perceptions. For example, whether a halfway house in proximity actually lowers property values is not the issue, but whether residents *perceive* this as a social problem taps more succinctly into the Hobbesian ideal. Baron and Paisecki (1981) claimed that there are multiple realities regarding the true identity of the victim in community care situations. Because community homes are usually placed into communities by state or federal authorities, many community residents feel a sense of infringement on their basic human rights. In particular, the researchers are concerned with the long-term residents of the community. These long-term residents believe that they have worked hard to establish their surroundings and wish to assert control over their environment and over potential outside threats.

The concept of "multiple realities" applies to our studies of community members. In the case of Salvation City, people who had resided in the area for a long time were likely to respond that they supported some of the social programs in local halfway houses. However, there were often indications that they felt that, in dealing with community care near their residences, they were "helping to solve the problems of outsiders." Our qualitative efforts allowed us to look into the multiple definitions of the situation. Indeed, many of the community residents actually felt that the halfway houses provided revenue to the area and had mixed feelings about accepting them as part of the community. However, many also felt that the town had surpassed a critical mass and should stop allowing the establishment of additional houses in the area.

Considering the geographic nature of the halfway house, one possible solution to residents' perceived quality of life concerns might be to place halfway houses in or around areas that are not very desirable to local residents. For example, one of the halfway houses that we observed had been placed where a "crack house" used to be. There were no viable residences within 500 feet of the home, which was surrounded by empty lots.

During our research, there were several recurring complaints related to the perceived quality of life among community residents living near halfway houses. These are summarized for the reader in Figure 6.2.

FIGURE **6.2.** Common Complaints among Community Residents.

They attract outsiders. The populations served by most of these homes are not local residents.

They bring crime to the area.

They bring drugs to the area.

Because the residents of the houses are substance users, they increase the demand for drug use in the area.

Because relapse is common, the halfway house residents leave the halfway house only to stay in the area and get into more trouble.

Other towns receive the benefit of the drug treatment for the general population, but they fail to support the host towns in covering the costs of the residual infrastructural needs that the host towns require.

MODELING FOR A MORALLY SOUND HALFWAY HOUSE POLICY

Seeking to resolve interests of social justice and social policy, we have constructed a model. The model proposes appropriate policies that address methods of establishment for halfway houses within certain communities. The model begins with identifying the appropriate location for the operation of a halfway house. Such a model is concerned with locally unwanted land use, which refers to the establishment of facilities in communities where they are deemed appropriate and financially advantageous. Places in areas that no one wants or cares to invest in should be the focus for placement. The model includes interaction—both formal and informal contact between interested parties in the community. It can be facilitated by the use of tax incentive programs such as the state of Connecticut's PILOT (payment in lieu of taxes) program. And, it ends with a model of integrity assessment that is both rigorous and frequently used. What we propose is not exactly a new set of ideas. Indeed, much social policy regarding halfway houses currently develops in the way we suggest here, but a near-ideal model of halfway house planning is proposed here.

FIGURE **6.3.** A Model for Halfway House Policy.

Locally unwanted land use ® Informal interaction between concerned parties/community altruism ® "Payment in lieu of taxes" acts ® Integrity testing

---

An open discourse is required between neighborhood members and the parties that are involved in the building of halfway houses. These community conversations should be covered in media outlets, and we suggest a long preparation period between the time a halfway house is proposed and the time it is actually established. In other words, we feel that community conversations should be held before halfway house operations begin. We feel that such discourse should cover the topic of outsiders and resolve it in a way that makes the community feel empowered by the placement of the halfway house.

Of course, the model does not intend to end with integrity testing of the facility. Instead, we propose that the model be continuous and incorporate constant feedback from members of the community into a halfway house within their area. We feel that such empowerment would facilitate the greater good by increasing quality of life perceptions among community residents.

LOCALLY UNWANTED LAND USE (LULU)

There are many social justice issues that present obstacles to halfway house placement within communities. In particular, we are concerned about geographic siting of halfway houses in lower-income neighborhoods that do not want them. In theory, the placement of residential care facilities in upper-income neighborhoods is also frightening to the moral sensibilities of many people. Experience shows that any attempt to set up halfway houses in upper-income neighborhoods is likely to be blocked by residents or filibustered into oblivion in arbitration. Such an arrangement would not result in a halfway house being established and would hinder the greater good.

It would seem that facilitating the greater good is best accomplished by intentionally siting halfway houses in areas where they are less likely to face resistance from the community. We do not deny that such areas exist primarily in lower-income neighborhoods. We do not attempt to define such neighborhoods directly, but note that there are many characteristics that they share, such as a great deal of abandoned housing and available rental property.

When we attempt to envision the best locations for halfway houses, we frequently concentrate on the inner city, lower-income urban landscape. This implies that placing halfway houses primarily in low-income areas would better facilitate the greater good in a more practical way. We do, however, recognize potential pitfalls with this approach. For example, Bohon and Humphrey (2000) discussed the fact that lower-income communities are also more likely to organize to fight the growth of such services. However, the placement of community care facilities in lower-income areas is something that may be easier to overlook with practical policy that offers financial incentives.

Identifying potential halfway house sites is a task that is often relegated to agencies or organizations wishing to provide rehabilitation services. We feel that one of the ways that it is possible to reconcile communities with halfway houses is for agencies to focus on appropriate plots of land located within communities and to build halfway houses on them. There were indicators that Salvation City and its halfway house communities bore more than their fair share of these appropriate areas. Although neighboring (and more affluent) towns had correctional institutions and psychiatric hospitals, clients in those institutions rarely went out in the general public.

COMMUNITY/HALFWAY HOUSE INTERACTION

As noted above, during our research effort we discovered that that there were several common complaints among community residents regarding the placement of halfway house programs. We also discovered, in the case of Vision House, that a great deal of negative community

perceptions were offset by appropriate interaction between the establish-
ers of a halfway house and the community prior to the establishment of
the community care facility.

We propose that any future policies regarding halfway house placement involve aggressive attempts by social care providers to establish
groundwork for communication between members of the community
and the halfway house program. We feel that such discourse could offset some of the problems associated with halfway houses. One common
complaint about halfway houses among community members we interviewed was that halfway houses attract outsiders to the community. For
example, in Salvation City, there was a perception that the community
was acting as a servant to people from the outside looking for handouts.
The populations served by most these homes were not local residents.

In community discourse, concerns about halfway houses bringing
crime and drugs to the community should also be addressed. Many of the
people that we interviewed felt that because the residents of the houses
were substance users, they increased the demand for drug use in the area.
They feared that because relapse is common, the halfway house residents
would leave only to stay in Salvation City and get into more trouble.

At this point, we do not really have any clear vision of how community
discourse would carry itself out. However, we can use our Vision House
study as a model. As pointed out earlier, the founder of Vision House had
close ties with the community before the establishment of the halfway house.
He was not considered an outsider by the community. Such results could be
replicated if halfway house providers would make themselves open to community discussion before the establishment of the houses within communities. In this way, we propose that successful interactions could be forged.

Payment In Lieu of Taxes Acts (PILOT)

One step towards getting past LULU resistance is for governments to
recognize that some communities bear the brunt of providing a greater
good to society and should, therefore, receive some sort of compensation

for bearing the burden. In our research, we discovered that many states have enacted what are known as PILOT programs. The acronym PILOT stands for "payment in lieu of taxes," which refers to the use of federal or state funds to compensate local or state governments. In states that have enacted PILOT programs, payment is given to local or state governments in exchange for provisions of social services. These programs seek to reimburse individual areas for lost revenue from tax-exempt property. PILOT programs are aimed at all dimensions of social service delivery, including halfway houses and privately operated hospitals and schools.

Citizens and towns need to understand that PILOT money, although smaller than average tax revenues, can be used to replenish community coffers. In areas where there were vacant or condemned buildings, there would otherwise be no tax revenue at all and the town would suffer. Sadly, we found in our interviews that not many people knew what PILOT money was.

Such a solution directly addresses one of the problems that halfway houses face. General community giving to halfway houses, like that of many other charitable programs, is only seasonal. Halfway houses suffer the same fate as many charitable programs. People may feel charitable at certain times of the year, such as Christmas. Like many soup kitchens and homeless shelters, halfway houses do not depend on volunteers. Halfway houses operate year-round and require consistent funding toward rehabilitation efforts. A PILOT program would, ideally, speak to the charitable sensibilities of state and local governments and allow more resources to be allocated to social services such as halfway houses. PILOT programs also provide for social justice, as communities that operate these programs often do suffer declining property values. In addition, PILOT programs ensure compliance with standards of operations within halfway houses. Such programs, because of their accountability, also ensure that adequate staff are hired and that there is adequate provision given to halfway house residents. The PILOT funds act as a vested interest in the town, thereby giving the community incentives to ensure that the halfway houses are operated in an effective manner.

INTEGRITY

The last phase of our model stresses integrity. We suggest that states and towns begin to formulate policy that is conducive to the maintenance of rehabilitative programming in halfway houses. One possible alternative for policy makers would be to require periodic CPAI assessments of integrity, commissioned by individual departments of corrections and mental health. Indeed, we found that many states keep up with their halfway house systems on a periodic basis through commissioned reports. Unfortunately, these commissioned reports often fall short of true tests of program integrity. We found many commissioned reports on houses that were more concerned with reentry rates and relapse than with programming integrity. We found that the employment of the CPAI as an integrity-testing mechanism is often quite rare. At this point, we recommend that some social policy include research incentives calling for periodic commissioned reports on halfway houses, using the CPAI as an integrity-testing mechanism. At the institutional level, the state could enact policy to ensure high-quality programming.

Although the CPAI could be used to assess integrity at the institutional level, there is unfortunately no design for testing integrity at the community level. To this end, we recommend that states adopt a policy that sets the community in motion as a watchdog. Halfway house administrators and staff must work with communities instead of operating in dark shadows. On a final note, some policies could attempt to incorporate integrity through the infusion of PILOT money specifically aimed at facilitating halfway houses in terms of their ability to hire staff and provide physical resources. Such formulated policy can be implemented in a politically neutral manner to solve the social problem. We note that there are several criteria for measuring the success of halfway houses that could be useful in determining integrity as well. These are reduced substance abuse,

abstinence, reduced arrest records, employment, educational achieve-
ment, independent living, and less dependent living.

SUMMARY

We began this book by focusing on an issue related to the "greater good."
It has led to the conclusion that the greater good can be served without
causing distress among a few selected individuals. The properly operated
halfway house represents a public good due to its humane emphasis on
rehabilitating individuals. We discovered this through the process of inter-
viewing several halfway house residents, who indicated that the structured confines of the halfway house provided them with an opportunity
to get their lives in order. More often than not, halfway house interviewees pointed out that the halfway house was a place of recollection where
thoughts could be gathered. However, our concern was not only with these
individuals, but also with the community members that had to adapt to the
establishment of residential care facilities within their neighborhoods.

At some level, we acknowledge that halfway houses, as they are currently operated, are often perceived as a hindrance to the greater good.
In many interviews, we got an earful of complaints from community
members who were not friendly to either the idea of halfway houses or
to researchers daring enough to bring up the subject. Because informal
neighborhood activities and pleasantries exchanged among familiar faces
help build neighborhoods, recovery home residents are at a disadvantage
when developing those relationships. Moreover, more often than not halfway house residents are perceived as interlopers within the boundaries of
communities. Their transience affects community organization. Ideally, a
recovery home resident would not stay in the same location for a long
period of time. They would eventually go on to their own independent life
instead of subjecting themselves to the numerous rules associated with the
halfway house. Some residents also shared a distaste for how actual home
values were affected by the presence of a halfway house in their area.

One issue that must be addressed in the future is the *free-rider* issue.
Although halfway houses can benefit host communities, they were often

perceived as a source of outsiders. In many cases, there was a serious concern that social service providers were largely professional social service employees who made their living in Salvation City and then took their money home to their families in neighboring towns. Numerous individuals in Salvation City stated that they supported recovery houses, stating that "[…] we take care of our own, but we don't need to be taking care of others." (Personal interview: Penny) This follows a long tradition of defining charity. Many critics of the concentration of recovery homes were quick to ask us "Where do you live?" as a litmus test for our right to voice an opinion. Indeed, we discovered that a halfway house was quite a controversial issue within the community.

Ultimately, we feel that communities can develop a collective interest in the common good if policies are enacted to ensure faith in that common good. Establishing healthy relations between communities and halfway houses is absolutely necessary to facilitate the well-being of community residents who live near halfway houses. This resolution of the respective needs of the halfway house and the community is difficult because both interested parties (the halfway house residents and the community residents) serve a certain good that can be justified without any apologies. Each interest is a noble interpretation.

Given the present condition of the economy, we see halfway houses as having no choice but to evolve into a viable option to traditional correctional, substance abuse, and mental health programming.

REFERENCES

Allen, H., Carlson, E., Parks, E., & Seiter, R.P. (1978). *Halfway houses: Program models*. Washington, DC: U.S. Department of Justice.

Anderson, E. (1999). *Code of the street: Decency, violence and the moral life of the innercity*. New York: Norton.

Andreas, P. (2000). *Border games: Policing the U.S.-Mexico divide*. Ithaca: Cornell University Press.

Andrews, D.A., & Bonta, J. (1994). *The psychology of criminal conduct*. Cincinnati: Anderson.

Andrews, D.A., Bonta, J., & Hoge, R.D. (1990). Classification for effective rehabilitation: Rediscovering psychology. *Criminal Justice and Behavior*, 17, 19–52.

Applegate, B.K., Cullen, F.T., & Fisher, B.S. (1997). Public support for correctional treatment: The continuing appeal of the rehabilitative ideal. *Prison Journal*, 77, 237–258.

Bailey, E. (1985, May 5). Residents object to halfway house as L.B. neighbor. Los Angeles Times, http://articles.latimes.com/1985-05-05/news/hl-8547_1_halfway-house retrieved October 11, 2010.

Ball, J.C., Shaffer, J.W., & Nurco, D. (1983). The day-to-day criminality of heroin addicts in Baltimore: A study in the continuity of offence rates. *Drug and Alcohol Dependence*, 12, 119–142.

Barnes, H.E., & Teeters, N.K. (1959). *New horizons in criminology*. Englewood Cliffs, NJ: Prentice Hall.

Baron, R.C., & Paisecki, J.R. (1981). The community versus community care. In R.D. Budson (Ed.), *New directions for mental health services: Issues in community residential care* (pp. 63–66). San Francisco: Jossey-Bass.

Baumohl, J. (1993). Inebriate institutions in North America, 1840–1920. In C.K.L. Warsh (Ed.), *Drink in Canada: Historical Essays* (pp. 92–114). Kingston: McGill-Queen's University Press.

Baumohl, J. (2000). Maintaining orthodoxy: The Depression-era struggle over morphine maintenance in California. *Contemporary Drug Problems, 27*, 17–75.

Baumohl, J. (2006). Inebriate institutions in North America, 1840–1920. *British Journal of Addiction, 85*(9), pp. 1187–1204.

Beha, J.A. II. (1976). Testing the functions and effect of the parole halfway house: One case study. *Journal of Criminal Law and Criminology, 67*, 335–350.

Belenko, S and Peugh, J. (2005). Estimating drug treatment needs among state prison inmates. *Drug and Alcohol 77*(3), 269-281.

Bellis, D.J. (1981). *Heroin and politicians: The failure of public policy to control addiction in America.* Greenwich, CT: Greenwood.

Bennett, T., & Wright, R. (2006). The impact of prescribing on the crimes of opioid abusers. *Addiction, 81*, 265–273.

Bentham, J. (2009 [1830]). *The Rationale of Punishment.* Amherst, NY: Prometheus Books.

Berlin, I. (1953). *The hedgehog and the fox: An essay on Tolstoy's view of history.* London: Weidenfeld and Nicolson.

Berlin, I. (2002). *Liberty.* [Henry Hardy (Ed.)]. New York: Oxford University Press.

Bohon, S., & Humphrey, C.R. (2000). Courting LULUs: Characteristics of suitor and objector communities. *Rural Sociology, 65*(3), 376–398.

Bonta, J., Rugge, T., Scott, T., Bourgon, G., & Yessine, A.K. (2008). Exploring the black box of community supervision. *Journal of Offender Rehabilitation, 47*, 248–270.

Byrne, J.M. (1990). The future of intensive probation supervision and the new intermediate sanctions. *Crime and Delinquency, 36*(1), 6–34.

Cade, J.F.J. (1949). Lithium salts in the treatment of psychotic excitement. *Medical Journal of Australia, 2*(36), 349–352.

Carpenter, M.D. (1978). A follow-up study of Berkeley House: A psychiatric halfway house. *International Journal of Social Psychiatry, 23,* 120–131.

Charlesworth, L. (2010). *Welfare's forgotten past: A socio-legal history of the poor law.* New York: Routledge.

Clemmer, D. (1940). *The Prison Community.* Boston: New York: Holt, Rinehart & Winston.

Cowan, H.S. (2003). NIMBY syndrome and public consultation policy: the implications of a discourse analysis of local responses to the establishment of a community mental health facility. *Health & Social Care in the Community. 11*(5), 379–386.

Colling-Chadwick, S. (1996). Comparison of intensive supervision probation and community corrections clientele. *Report of the Drug Control and Systems Improvement Program, Colorado Division of Criminal Justice, Denver, Colorado.*Connecticut Office of Policy and Management (2008). *State of Connecticut 2008 Annual Recidivism Study.* Hartford, CT: Connecticut Office of Policy and Management.

Costanza, S.E., & Kilburn, J.C., Jr., (2005). Symbolic security, moral panic and public sentiment: Toward a sociology of counterterrorism. *Journal of Social and Ecological Boundaries, 1,* 106–124.

Cowan, H.S. (2003). NIMBY syndrome and public consultation policy: The implications of a discourse analysis of local responses to the establishment of a community mental health facility. *Health & Social Care in the Community, 11*(5), 379–386.

Cullen, F.T. (1995). Assessing the penal harm movement. *Journal of Research in Crime and Delinquency. 32*(3), 338–358.

Dear, M. (1977). Impact of mental health facilities on property values. *Community Mental Health Journal, 13,* 150–157.

Dickens, C. (1986 [1843]). *A Christmas Carol*. New York: Bantam.

Doran, C.M. (2008). Economic evaluation of interventions to treat opiate dependence: A review of the evidence. *PharmoEconomics, 26*, 371–393.

Dowden, C., & Andrews, D.A. (1999). What works for female offenders: A meta-analytic review. *Crime & Delinquency, 45*, 438–452.

Durkheim, E. (1997 [1892]). *The Division of Labor in Society*. New York: Free Press.

Ehrenreich, B. (2008). *Nickel and dimed: On not getting by in America*. New York: Henry Holt.

Eynon, T.G. (1989). Building community support. *Corrections Today, 51*, 148–152.

Farber, S. (1986). Market segmentation and the effects of group homes for the handicapped on residential property values. *Urban Studies, 23*, 519–525.

Freudenburg, W. R., & Pastor, S.K. (1992). NIMBYs and LULUs: Stalking the syndromes. *Journal of Social Issues, 48*(4), 39–61.

Gandossy, Taylor. (2010, February 1). Trial stirs painful memories of brutal home invasion. *CNN*. Retrieved from http://www.cnn.com.

Gendreau, P., & Andrews, D.A. (1996). *Correctional Program Assessment Inventory (CPAI) 6th Edition*. Saint John, New Brunswick: University of New Brunswick Press.

Gendreau, P., Goggin, C., & Smith, P. (1999). The forgotten issue in effective correctional treatment: Program implementation. *International Journal of Offender Therapy and Comparative Criminology, 43*, 180–187.

Gendreau, P., Little, T., & Goggin, C. (1996). A meta-analysis of the predictors of adult offender recidivism: What works? *Criminology, 34*, 575–607.

Goffman, E. (1961). Asylums: Essays on the social situation of mental patients and other inmates. New York: Anchor Books.

Goffman, E. (1963). *Stigma: Notes on the management of spoiled identity*. New York: Simon & Schuster.

Gossop, M., Trakada, K., Stewart, D., & Witton, J. (2005). Reductions in criminal convictions after addiction treatment: 5-year follow-up. *Drug and Alcohol Dependency, 79*, 295–302.

Granovetter, M.S. (1973). The strength of weak ties. *American Journal of Sociology, 78*, 1360–1380.

Gray, C.M., C.J. Conover, T.M. Hennessey. 1978. Cost effectiveness of residential community corrections: An analytical prototype. *Evaluation Review, 2*, 378–399.

Grygier, T., B. Nease, and C. Staples Anderson. 1970. An exploratory study of halfway houses. *Crime & Delinquency, 16*(3), 280-291.

Gumrukcu, P. (1968). The efficacy of a psychiatric halfway house: A three-year study of a therapeutic residence. *Sociological Quarterly, 9*, 374–386.

Gusfield, J.R. (1986). *Symbolic crusade: Status politics and the American temperance movement* [2nd edition]. Urbana, IL: University of Illinois Press.

Hall, K.T., & Applebaum, P.S. (2002). The origins of commitment for substance abuse in the United States. *Journal of the American Academy of Psychiatric Law, 30*, 33–45.

Hardwood, S.A. 2003. Environmental justice on the streets: Advocacy planning as a tool to contest environmental racism. *Journal of Planning and Education Research, 23*, 24–38.

Harer, M.D. (1995). Recidivism among federal prisoners released in 1987. *Journal of Correctional Education, 46*, 98–128.

Hart, T., Callie, M., Rennison, C., & Gibson, C. (2005). Revisiting respondent "fatigue bias" in the national crime victimization survey. *Journal of Quantitative Criminology, 21*, 345–363.

Hartmann, D.J., & Friday, P.C. (1994). Residential probation: A seven-year follow up study of halfway house discharges. *Journal of Criminal Justice, 22,* 503–515.

Hetz-Burrell, N.H., & English, K. (2006). *Community corrections in Colorado: A study of program outcomes and recidivism, FY00–FY04. Report of the Office of Research and Statistics, Division of Criminal Justice, Colorado Department of Public Safety.*

Higginbotham, P. (2006). *Workhouses of the North.* Gloucester, U.K.: The History Press.

Hitchcock, H.C., Stainback, R.D., & Roque, G.M. (1995). Effects of halfway house placement on retention of patients in substance abuse aftercare. *American Journal of Drug & Alcohol Abuse, 21, 379–390.*

Hubbard, R.L., Flynn, P.M., Craddock, S.G., & Fletcher, B.W. (2001). Relapse after drug treatment. In F.M. Tims, C.G. Leukefeld, & J.J. Platt (Eds.), *Relapse and Recovery in Addictions* (pp. 109–121). New Haven, CT: Yale University Press.

Hughes, P. (1977). *Behind the wall of respect: Community experiments in heroin addiction control.* Chicago: University of Chicago Press.

Hunter, S., & Leyden, K.M. (1995). Beyond NIMBY: Explaining opposition to hazardous waste facilities. *Policy Studies Journal,* 23, 601–620.

Innes, C.A. (1993). Recent public opinion in the United States toward punishment and corrections. *The Prison Journal.* 73(2), 220–236.

Janzen, R.A. (2001). *The rise and fall of Synanon: A California utopia.* Baltimore: Johns Hopkins University Press.

Jason, L.A., Davis, M.I., Ferrari, J.R., & Bishop, P.D. (2001). Oxford House: A review of research and implications for substance abuse recovery and community research. *Journal of Drug Education,* 31, 1–27.

Jensen, R. (2002). "No Irish need apply": A myth of victimization. *Journal of Social History,* 36, 405–429.

Johnson, M.P. (2006). Decision models for the location of community corrections centers. *Environmental Planning & Design*, 33, 393–412.

Jones, P.R. (1991). The risk of recidivism: evaluating the public safety implications of a community corrections program. *Journal of Criminal Justice*, 19, 1, 49–66.

Kalinich, D.B., & Stojkovic, S. (1987). Contraband: The basis for legitimate power in a prison social system. *Journal of Crime & Justice*, 12, 435–451.

Kelly, C.E., & Welsh, W.N. (2008). The predictive validity of the level of service inventory—revised for drug-involved offenders. *Criminal Justice and Behavior*, 35, 819–831.

Kim, D.S. 2000. Another look at the NIMBY phenomenon. *Health & Social Work. 25*(2), 146–148.

Kraft, M.E., & Clary, B.B. (1991). Citizen participation and the NIMBY syndrome: Public response to radioactive-waste disposal. *The Western Political Quarterly, 44*, 299–328.

Krause, J.D. (1991). Community opposition to correctional facility siting: Beyond the "NIMBY" explanation. *Humboldt Journal of Social Relations, 17*, 239–262.

Kuno, E., Rothbard, A.B., Averyt, J.M., & Culhane, D.P. (2000). Homelessness among persons with severe mental illness in an enhanced community-based mental health system. *Psychiatric Services*, 51, 1012–1016.

La Vigne, N.G. (2010). Statement by Nancy G. La Vigne at a hearing on halfway home to the district: the role of halfway houses in reducing crime and recidivism in the nation's capital. House of Representatives Oversight and Government Reform Subcommittee on Federal Workforce, Postal Service, and the District of Columbia.

Latessa, E.J. (2004). The challenge of change: Correctional programs and evidence based practices. *Criminology & Public Policy, 3*, 547–560.

Levine, H.G. (1978). The discovery of addiction: Changing conceptions of habitual drunkenness in America. *Journal of Studies on Alcohol*, *15*, 493–506.

Listwan, S.J., M. Colvin, D. Hanley and D. Flannery. 2010. Victimization, social support, and psychological well-being: A study of recently released prisoners. *Criminal Justice and Behavior, 37*(10), 1140–1159.

Longmate, N. (2003). *The Workhouse*. London: Random House.

Lowenkamp, C.T., & Latessa, E.J. (2005). Developing successful reentry programs: Lessons learned from the "what works" programs. *Corrections Today*, *67*(2), 72–77.

Lowenkamp, C.T., Latessa, E.J., & Holsinger, A.M. (2006). The risk principle in action: What have we learned from 13,676 offenders and 97 correctional programs? *Crime & Delinquency*, *51*, 77–93.

Lowenkamp, C.T., Latessa, E.J., & Smith, P. (2006). Does correctional program quality really matter? The impact of adhering to the principles of effective intervention. *Criminology & Public Policy*, *5*, 571–584.

Mariner, J. (2001). *No escape: male rape in U.S. prisons*. New York: Human Rights Watch.

Marshall, J.D. (1961). The Nottinghamshire Reformers and their contribution to the new poor law. *The Economic History Review 13*, 382–396.

Martin, S.S., Butzin, C.A., Saum, C.S., & Inciardi, J.A. (1999). Three-year outcomes of therapeutic community treatment for drug-involved offenders in Delaware: From prison to work release to aftercare. *The Prison Journal*, *79*, 292–320.

Martinson, R. (1974). What works? Questions and answers about prison reform. *The Public Interest*, *35*, 22–54.

Martin, S.S., C.A. Butzin, C.A. Saum, and J.A. Inciardi. 1999. Three-year outcomes of community treatment for drug-involved offenders in

Delaware: From prison to work release to aftercare. *The Prison Journal.* 79:294–320.

Marx, K. (1997 [1848]). *The Communist Manifesto.* New York: Penguin.

Matejczyk, A.P. (2001). Why not NIMBY? Reputation, neighbourhood organisation and zoning boards in a US. Midwestern city. *Urban Studies, 38*, 507–518.

Matthews, B., Jones-Hubbard, D., & Latessa, E.J. (2001). Making the next step: Using evaluability assessment to improve correctional programming. *The Prison Journal, 81*, 454–472.

Massey, D.S., & Denton, N. (1993). *American apartheid: Segregation and the making of the underclass.* Cambridge, MA: Harvard University Press.

Mead, G.H. (1934). *Mind, Self, & Society.* Chicago: University of Chicago Press.

Metraux, S., & Culhane, D.P. (2004). Homeless shelter use and reincarceration following prison release: Assessing the risk. *Criminology & Delinquency, 52(3), 504–517.*

Myers, L., & Bridges, S. (1995). Public discourse: Property rights, public good and NIMBY. In M. Silver & M. Melkonian (Eds.), *Contested terrain: Power, politics and participation in suburbia* (pp. 133–148). Westport, CT: Greenwood Press.

Orndoff, C. R. (1978). Transitional Housing. *Psychiatric Quarterly. 50, 4, 269–273.*

Petersilia, J. (1995). A crime control rationale for reinvesting in community corrections. *The Prison Journal. 75, 4, 479–496.*

Piat, M. (2000a). Becoming the victim: A study on community reactions towards group homes. *Psychiatric Rehabilitation Journal, 24(2),* 108–116.

Piat, M. (2000b). The NIMBY phenomenon: Community residents' concerns about housing for deinstitutionalized people. *Health & Social Work, 25*(2), 127–138.

Piquero, N.L. (2003). A recidivism analysis of Maryland's community probation program. *Journal of Criminal Justice, 31*, 295–307.

Poitras, C., Altimari, D. and Tuohy, L. (2007, October 28). Prelude to horror. *Hartford Courant.* http://articles.courant.com/2007-10-28/news/hc-petit-suspects-102807_1_steven-hayes-suspect-barbecue/10 (retrieved July 10, 2010).

Quinn, J.F. (2003). *Corrections: A concise introduction.* Prospect Heights, IL: Waveland Press.

Rabkin, J.G., Muhlin, G., & Cohen, P.W. (1984). What neighbors think: Community attitudes toward local psychiatric facilities. *Community Mental Health Journal, 20*, 304–312.

Reich, R., & Siegel, L. (1978). The emergence of the Bowery as a psychiatric dumping ground. *Psychiatric Quarterly, 50*, 191–201.

Reichel, P. (2002). *Corrections: Philosophies, practices, and procedures.* Boston: Allyn & Bacon.

Roberts, J.V. (1998). American attitudes about punishment: Myth and reality. In J. Petersilia (Ed.), *Community corrections: Probation, parole, and intermediate sanctions* (pp. 143–148). New York: Oxford University Press.

Rosenhan, D.L. (1973). On being sane in insane places. *Science, 179*, 250–258.

Rossi, P.M. (1978). Issues in the evaluation of human services delivery. *Evaluation Review, 2*, 573–599.

Schively, C. (2007). Future research understanding the NIMBY and LULU phenomena: Reassessing our knowledge base and informing future research. *Journal of Planning Literature, 21*, 255–266.

Scott, N.J., & Scott, R.A. (1980). The impact of housing markets on institutionalization. *Administration in Mental Health, 7,* 210–222.

Segal, S.P., J. Baumohl, and E.W. Moyles. 1980. Neighborhood types and community reaction to the mentally ill: A paradox of intensity. *Journal of Health and Social Behavior. 21*(4), *345–359.*

Seeman, M. (1963). Alienation and social learning in a reformatory. *American Journal of Sociology, 69,* 270–284.

Shepard, D.S., Larson, M.J., & Hoffman, N.G. (1999). Cost-effectiveness of substance abuse services: Implications for public policy. *Psychiatric Clinics of North America, 22,* 385–400.

Sherman, L.W., Gottfredson, D.C., MacKenzie, D.L., Eck, J., Reuter, P., & Bushway, S. (1998). *Preventing Crime: What works, what doesn't, what's promising.* Washington, D.C: National Institute of Justice.

Sigler, R.T., & Lamb, D. (1995). Community based alternatives to prison: How the public and court personnel view them. *Federal Probation, 59,* 5–9.

Silverman, I. (2001). *Corrections: A comprehensive view.* Belmont, CA.: Wadsworth Publishing.

Simourd, D., & Andrews, D.A. (1994). Correlates of delinquency: A look at gender differences. *Forum on Corrections Research, 6,* 26–31.

Skogan, W.G. (1990). *Disorder and decline: Crime and the spiral of decay in American neighborhoods.* Berkeley, CA: University of California Press.

Slack, P. (1990). *The English Poor Law, 1531 to 1782.* Cambridge, U.K.: Cambridge University Press.

Steffensmeier, D.J. (1986). *The fence: In the shadow of two worlds.* Lanham, MD: Rowman and Littlefield.

Stevens, Dennis J. (2005). *Community corrections: An applied approach.* Englewood Cliffs, NJ: Prentice Hall.

Substance Abuse and Mental Health Services Administration. (2003). New Freedom Commission on Mental Health, *Achieving the Promise: Transforming Mental Health Care in America, Final Report* (2003), Rockville, MD: Substance Abuse and Mental Health Services Administration.

Sutherland, E.H., Cressey, D.R., & Luckinbill, D.F. (1992). *Principles of criminology.* Dix Hills, N.J. General Hall.

Suzuki, A. (1995). The politics and ideology of non-restraint: The Case of Hanwell Asylum. *Medical History*, 39, 1–17.

Swartz, M.S., Swanson, J.W., Hiday, V.A., Borum, R., Wagner, R., & Burns, B.J. (1998).Violence and severe mental illness: The effects of substance abuse and nonadherence to medication. *American Journal of Psychiatry*, 155, 226–231.

Szasz, T.S. (1970). *The Manufacture of Madness: a comparative study of the Inquisition and the mental health movement.* New York: Harper & Row.

Takahashi, L.M. (1997). The socio-spatial stigmatization of homelessness and HIV/AIDS: Toward an explanation of the NIMBY syndrome. *Social Science and Medicine*, *45*(6), 903–914.

Takaki, R. (1993). *A different mirror: A history of multicultural America.* New York: Back Bay Books.

Thomas, C.W., & Foster, S.C. (1973). The importation model perspective on inmate social roles. *The Sociological Quarterly*, *14*, 225–234.

Travis, J. (2005). *But they all come back: Facing the challenges of prisoner reentry.* Boston, MA: Urban Institute Press.

Travis, J., & Visher, C.A. (2005). *Prisoner reentry and crime in America.* New York: Cambridge University Press.

Valverde, M. (1998). *Diseases of the will: Alcohol and the dilemmas of freedom.* New York: Cambridge University Press.

von Hirsch, A., Bottoms, A.E. Burney, E and. Wikström, P.O. (1999). *Criminal deterrence and sentence severity.* Oxford: Hart Publishing.

Walsh, C.L., & Beck, S.H. (1990). Recidivism among halfway house residents. *Journal of Criminal Justice, 15*(2), 137–149.

Walters, G.D. (2000). Spontaneous remission from alcohol, tobacco, and other drug abuse: seeking quantitative answers to qualitative questions. *American Journal of Drug and Alcohol Abuse. 26*(3), 443–460.

Ward, M. (2008, April 3). Halfway house solution: Build them prisons. *American-Statesman.* http://www.statesman.com/news/content/news/stories/local/04/03/0403halfway.html (retrieved October 22, 2010).

Warren, M.R. (2001). *Dry bones rattling: Community building to revitalize American democracy.* Princeton, N.J.: Princeton University Press.

Webster's. (2002). *Third new international dictionary of the English language unabridged.* Springfield, MA: Merriam-Webster.

Wexler, H.K., G.P. Falkin, and D.S. Lipton. 1990. Outcome evaluation of a prison therapeutic community for substance abuse treatment. *Criminal Justice and Behavior. 17*(1), 71–92.

Wieder, L.D. (1988). *Language and social reality.* Lanham, MD: University Press of America.

Wilson, W.J. (1987). *The truly disadvantaged: The inner city, the underclass, and public policy.* Chicago: University of Chicago Press.

Wilton, R.D. (2002). Colouring special needs: Locating whiteness in NIMBY conflicts. *Social & Cultural Geography, 3,* 303–321.

Wittenburg, A. (2008, May 28). Petit home demolished. *Record-Journal.* *http://www.myrecordjournal.com/latestnews/article_5ca3f01e-76f3-5592-9c36-080c824d8902.html* retrieved November 4, 2010.

Zimring, F.E. (1993). Drug treatment as a criminal sanction. *University of Colorado Law Review, 64,* 809–825.

INDEX